The career of Henry Youle Hind (1823-1908) has
assumed greater interest at a time when the
significance of early scientific exploration for
the development of Canada is being actively studied.
Hind was associated with the new body of professional
man - centred on Toronto engineers, surveyors,
architects - who founded the Canadian Institute in
1851, and he edited its journal for several years.
Then in 1857 and 1858-60 he was involved in expeditions to the Red River and to the Assiniboine and
Saskatchewan, expeditions stemming from high curiosity in the province of Canada about prospects of
development in the northwest; his reports, and
other publications based on them, have been rich
sources of first-hand information on the west Hind
saw and valuable examples of the development of
scientific observation in the mid 19th century.
He continued his descriptive undertakings with
writing on explorations in the Labrador. The latter
years of his scientific career were centred on
geology in the Maritime Provinces and his life
concluded in Windsor, N.S.
  W.L. Morton, with his usual narrative and descriptive skill, has added another work to his fine list
of studies of the west.

W.L. Morton has latterly been Professor of History
at the University of Manitoba.

W.L. MORTON

Henry Youle Hind
1823–1908

Canadian Biographical Studies
UNIVERSITY OF TORONTO PRESS
Toronto and Buffalo

©University of Toronto Press 1980
Toronto and Buffalo
Printed in Canada

ISBN 0-8020-3278-8

Canadian Cataloguing in Publication Data

Morton, William L., 1908 -
Henry Youle Hind 1823-1908

(Canadian biographical studies ; 7   ISSN 0045-4486)
Bibliography: p. 147
Includes index.
ISBN 0-8020-3278-8

1. Hind, Henry Youle, 1823-1908. 2. Geologists - Canada - Biography. 3. Explorers - Canada - Biography. I. Series.

QE22.H56M67   550'.92'4   C80-094421-6

This book has been published with the help of the block grant programs of the Canada Council and the Ontario Arts Council.

Frontispiece is from a photograph by Notman, reproduced in Frank Leslie's Illustrated Newspaper (New York), 26 February 1881

Contents

Foreword vii

Acknowledgements ix

I Young Scholar of Nottingham 3
II Scientist in the Making 13
III The Red River Expedition 1857 29
IV The Assiniboine and Saskatchewan Expedition 1858–1860 58
V The Search for Fame 1860–1864 83
VI Failure in New Brunswick 1864–1866 99
VII The Last Controversy and the Long Peace 113

Notes 127

Bibliography 147

Index 155

Foreword

This volume is the seventh and concluding volume to be published in the series Canadian Biographical Studies. The series was designed to be an alliance of the *Dictionary of Canadian Biography/Dictionnaire biographique du Canada* by offering volumes which would be an anticipation of or accompaniment to the work of the larger project. Its small volumes, intended to interest a range of readers, sought to fill a gap in knowledge of figures who seemed often to be secondary in Canada's story, and yet are of importance for an understanding of her social, educational, and economic as well as political history.

At the time the series was begun, the DCB/DBC was proceeding at a slow pace through the 18th century and in a decade or two of the 19th. Its programme of work was not long afterward to be greatly enlarged and its schedule advanced when increased support through the Canada Council and then the Social Sciences and Humanities Research Council of Canada became available. It has now published volumes for the years up to 1800 and for the years 1861-1880; volumes to fill in the gaps up to 1900 are in preparation. The DCB/DBC was thus immersed in the process of covering the record for the 19th century and has concentrated its resources upon that task.

It is a pleasure to present this volume, whose publication has been delayed by a complication of factors but whose appropriateness to current interests in historiography will be evident. Professor Morton offers yet another of his skilful analyses of the interacting of personality and event and as well another of his fine evocations of the West.

Thanks and appreciation are due to the editors of the series, Alan Wilson and André Vachon, for their great efforts on its behalf over most of its life. Only those who have taken charge of a series know the bewilderments as well as the accomplishments of such an undertaking; readers of the volumes in the series, listed below, have reason to be grateful to the editors for the contribution they make to the understanding of our history through, in Alan Wilson's words, 'the careers and ideas - acknowledged, but often unrecognized - of Canadians of many ranks and diverse times.'

The Publishers

1. John Strachan 1778-1867
   J.L.H. Henderson

2. Roland Michel Barrin de La Galissonière 1693-1756
   Lionel Groulx

3. John Sandfield Macdonald 1812-1872
   Bruce W. Hodgins

4. Henry Alline 1748-1784
   J.M. Bumsted

5. The Denison Family of Toronto 1792-1925
   David Gagan

6. H.H. Stevens 1878-1973
   Richard Wilbur

7. Henry Youle Hind 1823-1908
   W.L. Morton

Acknowledgments

As apparently only scattered and fugitive letters of Henry Youle Hind survived, the quest for information on his life and accomplishments was both widespread and uncertain. I have to thank for much help in the quest Mr W. David Crane and Mr and Mrs Charles Hanson of Nottingham, the Public Reference Library of Nottingham, the Metropolitan Toronto Library and the Ontario Archives, Mr John A. Duncanson of Toronto, Miss M. Hind of Windsor, the Public Archives of Nova Scotia, the New Brunswick Museum of Saint John, the Public Archives of Canada, and the Library of Queen's University. I owe thanks also to Trent University for a term's leave, to the Canada Council for a research and travel grant, to Professor Alan Wilson, until recently general editor of the series in which this biography appears, for advice and guidance, and to Miss Francess Halpenny of the *Dictionary of Canadian Biography*. Faults and errors are of course of my own doing.

W.L. Morton

HENRY YOULE HIND

1 Young Scholar of Nottingham

Henry Youle Hind was born on 1 June 1823 in St. Mary's Gate, Nottingham, the third son of Thomas Hind, lace manufacturer, and his wife Sarah Youle Hind.[1] The time was the reign of George IV; the Tory reaction still continued, but the Radical movement was gathering force. Nottingham itself was a Radical town, even if overlooked by the fortress residence of the Duke of Newcastle on the rock, by the nearby seat of Lord Wollerton, and by distant Belvoir Castle of the Manners.

To gain some insight into Hind's career and personality requires understanding of the city and shire of Nottingham. Everyone knows the shire as the country of Robin Hood, and the city and castle as the base of the wicked Sheriff, prototype of the harassed bureaucrats of today. Some remember that it was at Nottingham that Charles I raised the royal standard in 1641. In 1823 Nottingham outwardly remained in many ways the medieval city of its famous Goose Fair and of the Jerusalem Inn at the foot of the Castle rock. But the genuine character of the city and shire had little to do with medieval romance, or indeed with lost causes of any kind.

Nottingham city, which represents the shire well, is in the northern Midlands, and by geography was

destined for a part in the Industrial Revolution.
Indeed in that great change Nottingham might claim
to have led the way. For in the parish of Calverton,
north of Nottingham, a parson of the Church of
England, the Rev. William Lee, invented in 1589
the stocking frame, a machine for knitting hose.
The hosiery trade came to settle in Nottingham.
The city in time attracted other machine industry.
There in 1769 Richard Arkwright erected his first
spinning frame; there came James Hargrave, driven
with his spinning jenny from Birmingham. These
were the great examples of a long series of in-
genious, often minute, inventions in weaving and
spinning, knitting and bobbin lacemaking. Out of
this complex of mechanical ingenuity developed in
all its variety the lace trade in which Hind's
father spent his life.[2]

The impression one derives from the history of
the city of 40,000 people in 1821 is thus one of
invention, industry, and drive. The people of
Nottingham were aggressive, curious, restless people
who incessantly improved the crafts by which they
and their city lived, and never missed a chance to
push their products in the markets of the world.
They also sent their youth abroad, such as Dr. J.
J. Bigsby, or Hind himself, who was to follow
Bigsby's footsteps in Canadian geology, or Harriet
Thompson whom Hind was to meet at Fairford Mission
near Lake Manitoba during his exploration of the
northwest.[3] But so hard were the machines driven
by their masters that Nottingham was also the turbulent centre of Luddism, the breaking of the
machines by the unemployed thrown out of work by
improvements; Lord Byron, who defended the Luddites
before the Lords in one of his rare acts of humanity,
had his home at Newstead Abbey just to the north of
the city.

Nottingham overlooks the Vale of Trent from the
north. It rests on two prominences; to the west

is the sandstone outcrop on which the Castle stands; to the east is the elevation where the dwellings and shops of the lace makers and lace merchants were; between lies a depression which is the gateway to the north of England and gave the city its strategic importance. In the heart of the lace district, fronting on St. Mary's Gate, with its rear opening on Stoney Street, Thomas Hind, Henry's father, had his lace warehouse, outbuildings, garden, stables, and washhouse. He lived above these premises, the whole on some 1,700 square yards of land in one of the most congested city areas of England.

Thomas Hind had no distinguished background - Hind was a common name in Nottinghamshire, and in fact could be found all over England[4] - but he had been a well-to-do and rising manufacturer since the early years of the century. From at least 1823 to 1837 he was among the leaders of industry in his city and probably was known even in London.[5] When a Chamber of Commerce was established in Nottingham in May 1835, he was one of its fifteen directors.[6] Henry's mother, Sarah Youle, came from a somewhat different background. Her family lived in Gainsborough, Lincolnshire, and her two brothers, George and Henry Youle, were merchants who imported timber by the Trent river and canal and settled in Nottingham.[7] From this chance of business came the marriage of which Henry was born. Southward from Thomas Hind's premises down St. Mary's Gate stands St. Mary's parish church. There on 6 June 1823 Hind was christened into the Church of which he was to remain a life-long faithful member.

The church and the church yard might be quiet but they were set on the edge of the throbbing lace district, crowded with narrow streets in blocks, both square and irregular, on the low hill above the great market-place and across from the bluff height of the Castle rock. Here from dawn to dusk could be heard the incessant thudding of the bobbinnet machine and 'the thump and running click of the stocking frames.'[8] The yards of lace, *blonde de cambrai* and white, went to the warehouses of the merchants, and the carts lumbered with their bales down the flagged streets to the Trent. In house after house were weavers' garrets on the top floors, with long windows to light the looms and the fine tissues of lace. Hind, with his two older brothers, Thomas and James Fisher, one younger, William, and his sister Sarah, grew up in the congestion of this busy lace district and its unceasing industry. He was raised above his father's warehouse, but he was reared in comfortable circumstances, a child of a hard-working, thrifty, self-made businessman. It was a comfortable environment, but neither an idle nor a luxurious one. The restless energy, the individual enterprise Hind was to display all his life until his last years came from the circumstances of his birth and childhood.

The times of his boyhood were also tense. Industrial England had been striving for change since Waterloo, and by 1830 change became possible. The Tories, forced to repeal the Test and Corporation acts, and to grant the vote to Irish Roman Catholics throughout the United Kingdom, had nevertheless given way to the Whigs under Earl Grey and to the demand for electoral reform. Nottingham had reason within itself to be radical: pressed between the unbuilt on lands of the Corporation of the borough and the Duke of Newcastle's and Lord Wollerton's estates; with fierce competition among employers and workers alike; with bad housing and bad sanitation in working class quarters; with its two main industries, hosiery and lacemaking, dependent on the fashions and prosperity of distant markets in Germany and the United States.[9] In national politics to 1832 it was Whig, as a corporation borough electing its MPs, but the temper of its working class was radical, with a tradition of riot from 1776 to the 1840s.[10] That temper was to burst out in its greatest eruption in 1831. In October came the news of the defeat of the second Reform Bill, greatly helped by the opposition of the then Duke of Newcastle, and the mob stormed up the rock and sent the Castle up in towering flame. One may suppose that on the cool autumn night the young Hind watched from Mary Gate across the housetops of the lower district as the most spectacular act of violence in the slow passage of the Reform Bill lighted up the angry city and the woods and fields for miles around. This harsh and restless background of Hind's childhood may have contributed to the harsh and restless strain that underlay Hind's outwardly mild and calm temper.

The boy, while still only fourteen years of age, was also to meet in 1837 the rigours of business life. The great depression of that year fell with especial weight on Nottingham and particularly on the makers of lace.[11] The market collapsed. In the second half of the year notices of bankruptcy proceedings began to appear in the local papers. Thomas Hind's name was not among them, but on 16 June the *Nottingham Review* had advertised the sale at the Flying Horse Inn of the

> Mansion fronting on Mary Gate, lately occupied by Mr. Thomas Hind, with the Lace Warehouse, Outbuildings and Gardens adjoining.
> Also the Stables and Coachhouse fronting Stoney Street and communicating with a Garden with the above property, and a piece of ground opposite to the Mansion.

The whole, it was noted, was 'suitable for valuable buildings.' Thomas Hind presumably satisfied his creditors, but he was not well-to-do thereafter.[12] He retired from business, and moved his family outside the town to Belvoir Terrace in adjoining Sneinton overlooking the valley of the Trent. The modest Georgian house is now run down. There Thomas died in 1845. In these straitened circumstances, Henry had to rely on himself and his education. He must make his way by his own efforts. It was no unusual fate for a Nottingham man to face; in Hind it gave an edge to the competitive temper he had acquired from his background.

The same quality of self-dependence appears in his formal education. Hind brought to study and to what is now called science the drive, the ingenuity, the acquisitive self-assertion that marked his townsmen. He received his education in part by private tuition. He also had a formal schooling, which was the ground work for his later career as a scientist and writer. This he received at the Free Grammar School of Nottingham, in Stoney Street a few yards from his father's door. It was an old foundation dating from 1513. As the name 'Grammar' indicated, it taught classics, together with mathematics and penmanship. Scholars were nominated by the Corporation of Nottingham and on the whole a boy's parents had to be of some standing for him to win a nomination.

The school, like many others, had become backward and to some degree corrupt by 1800, but the general movement for reform affected it also in the 1820s. Changes set in as required by the citizens and the times, in the direction of more emphasis on writing and mathematics, even commercial subjects. In 1833 a new headmaster, Mr. William Butler, a graduate of Cambridge University, greatly improved the tone and quality of the school.[13] He deplored the effect of the changes on the classics department, and by teaching classics himself did much to keep up the original character of the school. Butler is the one known personal influence on Hind, and it would seem that what scholarly training Hind possessed came from him. The personal impress of the headmaster could be immediate and considerable because the total enrolment of the school was from eighty to one hundred pupils, with four masters including the head. As boys were taken in at the age of eight, it may be that Hind entered in 1831 and spent six years in attendance, four under Butler.

In the classics, history (both Roman and English) was Hind's favourite subject, as it was for at least the brighter boys. Three boys led in the school from 1833 to 1838: W.R. Stevenson; Hind himself; and his cousin John Russell Hind, son of John Hind, brother of Thomas Hind and fellow lace manufacturer. Stevenson graduated at the University of London and became a prominent Baptist minister in that city. John Hind, after a brilliant career at Cambridge, gained a post at the Royal Observatory, Greenwich, and became a distinguished astronomer - secretary, then president, of the Royal Astronomical Society, Fellow of the Royal Society, and a Doctor of Laws. Henry Hind held his own in this company; the historian of the school describes him as 'a clever boy at School, excellent in History, also an enthusiastic entomologist.' Stevenson, to whom we owe our one clear glimpse of Hind as a schoolboy, notes that, 'Harry Hind was a bright, clever boy, the competitor with whom I had the sharpest struggle in the last contest for the History prize. He was scientific in his tastes and at that time an entomologist. I remember him taking me to his house in Belvoir Terrace, Sneinton, and showing me a beautiful collection he had made of butterflies and other insects.'[14] It is a familiar scene of Victorian boyhood.

One may note the formal training in history, which helps to explain Hind's skill in marshalling evidence in his later writing. His own enthusiasm for entomology would be useful on the Western

prairies. The hint of competition sounds through
Mr. Butler's school, and certainly it was necessary
for Hind to be keen to acquire an education. He
was the third son of a retired manufacturer whose
means had dwindled. Thomas, his eldest brother,
amiable and weak, had gained a position as clerk
in the Nottingham Savings Bank.[15] The second son,
James Fisher Hind, had gone into the lace trade.
Henry may have thought of entering business but
in 1837 he did what was for an English boy an unusual thing: he went to study at the forerunner
of the Königliche Handelshochschule, the Oeffentliche
Handelslehranstalt at Leipzig. Yet a boy from
Nottingham, which had ties by the lace trade with
Germany, might do so appropriately.

This institution, begun only in 1831 and the
first of its kind, was the outcome of the royal,
or state, promotion of higher education in place
of church patronage, and of the new humanism that
was transforming education in Germany.[16] It reflected also the vigour and ambition of a great
commercial city through whose famous fair Nottingham
lace found its way to eastern Europe. The
Handelslehranstalt, a commercial college, offered
an apprentice's education in the technological
arts.[17] There Hind remained until 1839. He acquired German, of course, and may have gained some
knowledge of chemistry. There too he may just
possibly have studied geology, aided by private
reading in the works of Alexander von Humboldt,
whose writings influenced Hind as a scientist and
an explorer.[18]

Hind remained in Leipzig only two years, however,
and returned to England. If he had had thoughts
of a career in business, he must have given them
up. Did he disappoint his father in this matter?
A distinctly businesslike and aggressive attitude
appears nevertheless in his later free-lance scientific work which he seemed to regard as a manufacturer

did his wares. In Nottingham, Hind studied privately for some four more years with Mr. Butler, and then went up to Cambridge.[19] On 26 May 1843 he was admitted to Caius College, but on 9 October migrated to Queen's, Mr. Butler's college, where he was admitted as a scholar. For reasons unknown, he resided only one year, and thus left without a degree.[20] In 1845 he spent four months in France to increase his proficiency in French.[21] His stay also gave him some knowledge of the French educational system. In 1846 he returned to England, and shortly thereafter sailed to North America. Why, or how, he went is not known; it is tempting to suppose he sailed on a merchant ship laden with lace for the elegant city of New Orleans. He himself recorded that he travelled on the prairies of Louisiana and Texas, an interesting introduction to America for an explorer of the Canadian Northwest.[22] From the southern United States he went to what was then the Province of United Canada, and settled in Toronto, again for reasons unknown. He was there by the winter of 1846-1847 as revealed by his publishing an article on a meteorological 'halo' in March 1847. The new world had already provoked his scientific interests.[23]

The record of Hind's life from 1837 to 1846 is thus bare of detail and lacking in explanation. No reason appears for his departure from Leipzig. From 1839 to 1843 he must have lived at home. Perhaps a small legacy following his father's death in 1845 paid for the time in France and the journey to Canada. Why he should have come to Canada is a mystery. His studies, leading to no degree, and with perhaps no formal study in chemistry and geology, may today seem lacking in direction, although Hind, like other eminent Victorians without degrees, was beyond question a well-educated man.

He was educated enough, at any rate, to impress the Superintendent of Education in Canada West, the Rev. Egerton Ryerson. Ryerson's biographer calls it 'a master stroke' when, in October 1847, Hind was appointed second master to teach science and mathematics at the provincial Normal School, Toronto.[24] Hind, it seemed, had done very well for a young man of twenty-four.

II Scientist in the Making

The Normal School at Toronto was a new venture in Canadian education. Recommended by Egerton Ryerson to the Council of Public Instruction, which had oversight of the school system, it was meant to provide a supply of trained teachers for the rapidly increasing schools of Canada West. The post to which Hind had been appointed was, therefore, a significant one, and might lead to the exercise of great influence in the educational system of the growing community.

The headmaster was Thomas Jaffray Robertson, a graduate of Trinity College, Dublin, who had been head inspector of the Irish National Schools. He had been nominated for the post in Canada West by the commissioners of the Irish National Schools, and it was his experience of that system, in which secular instruction was general and religious teaching denominational, that helped to win him the appointment. Hind was appointed for a similar reason, the variety of his experience, as a historian of the Normal School makes clear: 'With Mr. Robertson was associated Henry Youle Hind, formerly scholar of Queen's College, Cambridge, and latterly [*sic*] a student at the Royal Commercial College at Leipzig, and who was familiar with the methods of teaching in France and Germany.' Evidently Hind, or his sponsors, had made the most of his travels and studies and had satisfied Ryerson that the lack of a degree and only three years of formal study were not impediments to professional usefulness. His rank and duties corresponded with their confidence: Hind was second master and lecturer in 'Mathematics, Natural Philosophy and Agricultural Chemistry.'[1]

Hind, at any rate, was to justify his appointment. When the school opened on 1 November 1847, he began perhaps the happiest, if not the most exciting, five years of his life. Hind was third speaker at the opening, after Ryerson and Robertson, and gave a lecture on his own subjects, natural philosophy, agricultural chemistry, and mathematics. It was thought perhaps rather dry by the historian of the school, but that impression was not shared by the *British Colonist* or the *Globe*, both of which said that it was excellent. The *Globe*, however, warned Robertson and Hind that learning was not enough, and that 'fire and zeal' would be required to inspire their pupils and every common school in the country, and the praise of the *Colonist*'s reporter suggests Hind had clearly grasped that he must give his teaching a strong utilitarian bent. Perhaps the reason for approving Hind was that he had seen their points and Robertson had not; certainly he was reported to have been 'loudly applauded' while Robertson received only 'warm applause.' As this is the first personal glimpse we have had of Hind since he displayed his collection of butterflies at Belvoir Terrace, it is worth quoting the account of his speech despite the pompous style:

> Mr. Hind followed Mr. Robertson in an elaborate address on the subjects of Natural Philosophy, Agricultural Chemistry, and Mathematics. The polished elegance of the style, the easy and

attractive manner in which it was delivered, the deep research it showed, and the extensive knowledge evinced therein - and this withal with a plainness that commended itself to the meanest capacity - were the marks of general commendation after the address was completed; and while in course of delivery had its recognition in a silence as expressive as it was truthful.

The young man from Nottingham had obviously caught and held his audience, and indeed the address is well written if a trifle poetic in the transitions.[2]

Nothing is known in detail of how Hind discharged his responsibilities in mathematics and the sciences, or of how he was regarded by his students. It is apparent, however, that he incurred no serious, if any, criticism, and he was strongly supported by a large part of the Council of Public Instruction.[3] The period is marked, moreover, by the appearance of his first two publications. Both were undistinguished but useful essays. The first, printed in Toronto in 1850, was entitled *Lectures on Agricultural Chemistry*, and was made up of the lectures Hind had written for delivery in the Normal School. Three hundred copies were sent to the agricultural societies of Upper Canada, 60 to the Council of Public Instruction, and 25 to the Teacher's Institute. Set out as lectures with summaries, the work was suitable for use by teachers and speakers. It was addressed to Canadian conditions and kept in mind 'that mixed system [of farming] which universally prevails in this country.' The pamphlet is a good example of science put to the service of the community.

So also is the second essay, published in 1851, *A Comparative View of the Climate of Western Canada* ('western' in the then sense of the term). It is chiefly an exposition of how the influence of the lakes tempered the climate of the 'peninsula' - as what is now southwestern Ontario was then called - and, so Hind alleged, made it more favourable to farming than the adjoining wheat-growing parts of the United States. The agricultural, and horticultural, aim of the lecture as well as its political tone were clear.

Hind, it would seem, was taking his role as science master with proper seriousness. But nothing more is known of his work at the Normal School, except that there is an indication some members of the Council of Public Instruction desired in 1851 to make Hind the equal of Robertson. The latter apparently had not convinced all concerned of his right to the style and authority of headmaster.[4] Nothing more came of this unless it affected Hind's decision to leave the school in 1853. But it is perhaps to be noted for future recollection as the first indication of what was to recur, Hind's difficulty in working under superiors, or perhaps his misfortune in those who were his superiors. No one of Hind's capacity, it would seem, could have been entirely happy under Robertson, who in fact left the school in 1853.

Hind, however, had had other things to occupy him. On 7 February 1850, at York Mills, he married Katharine Cameron, second daughter of the late Lieutenant-Colonel Duncan Cameron, C.B., of the 79th Highlanders and a veteran of Quatre Bras.[5] Nothing is known of how the couple met. What is evident is that theirs was a love match and resulted in a happy marriage; Mrs. Hind was an invariably kind and jolly person who offset the austerity and sharpness that overlay Hind's own warmth of personality. It was also a fruitful marriage. Their first child, a son, Thomas Francis Neil, was born in 1851. The Hind family were now settled in Toronto. Four other sons and two daughters were to be added by 1863. The family lived first on Adelaide Street west of Bay, then on Spadina Avenue, and then on

Patrick Street, new areas of the small city of that day.⁶ That Patrick Street was still somewhat rural in the 1850s is revealed by Hind's remark that he grew melons there.⁷

In 1851 another event had revealed both that Hind had kept ties with his old home in Nottingham and that he was adding to roots he was sinking in his new home. Sometime in 1851, apparently, his brother, William G.R. Hind, his junior by ten years and the last of the seven children of Sarah Youle Hind, joined him in Toronto. He was, like the eldest son, Thomas, a weakling of the family, and given to drink, and perhaps his mother thought a new country and Henry's supervision would help him find himself, as to some degree at least it did. William had studied art in London and Europe and in 1852 became drawing master at the Normal School for five years.⁸ As Henry was to do through his writings, William by his painting was to help open to Canadians the wide horizons beyond the parishes and villages along the St. Lawrence and the Lakes.

It is true that by 1851 Canada was stirring and no part more than Toronto. The political turmoil of the late 1830s and 1840s had given way to responsible government and the rough but good-natured party controversies of the 1850s, with all parties accepting the rules of constitutional government and the doctrine of progress. The slow drift of the timber raft and the placid drag of the canal barge no longer set the pace of Canadian life; nor did even the brisk trot of carriole and cutter. The railway was coming and in a few years the tempo was set by locomotives shrieking along at all of 25 miles an hour, winter as well as summer. By the middle of the decade, with the revival of business after a depression in 1847, the prospect of increased trade with the United States by means of a reciprocity treaty, and, above all, the demand for wheat created when the Crimean War closed the ports of the Black Sea, the province of Canada saw the greatest boom it was ever to know. As the fifties waned, immigrants poured in; businesses multiplied, and Canadians began to look around and abroad for new opportunities. In Toronto, led by George Brown's *Globe*, some - old Hudson's Bay Company men and new businessmen - began to look to the Northwest, still governed by the company and still British on a continent in which the United States had advanced to the Pacific by 1848.

All this expansion was greatly to affect Henry Youle Hind, but only after some time. Meanwhile other events were to help advance his claim to be a scientist and set him on the way to the Northwest. One was the founding in 1849 of the Canadian Institute. When it began, the society revealed the presence, and set out to serve the interests, of a new body of professional men, engineers, surveyors, architects, in Toronto. Some of the founders were men later to be well known in Canada: John Stoughton Dennis, surveyor; F.W. Cumberland, engineer and architect; Sandford Fleming, civil engineer. It was a brave effort by a few young men, carried out at a critical moment when Fleming with only one companion held the necessary meeting to organize.[9]

The new society was, however, to languish and Hind had no reason to be interested in the original institute. But in 1851 it was reorganized and its interests broadened to include both the professions and science, and even literature. A royal charter was sought and obtained. The Royal Canadian Institute, with William E. Logan, director of the Geological Survey of Canada, as its first president to give its launching the prestige of his already considerable name, then set out on a century of service to science in Canada.[10]

As reorganized, the Canadian Institute was of great interest to Hind. Its general character suited his own broad scientific tastes. Meetings would bring him into contact with other men of similar concerns and with the professional engineers of Toronto and the trained scientists of University College of the University of Toronto. He became a member in December 1851, and in December 1852 he was elected a member of the council and second vice-president.[11] At the institute's second annual conversazione, in 1851, he spoke on 'The Climate of this Part of the Province,' the address presumably being the substance of his pamphlet, *A Comparative View*.[12] In August 1852 the institute began a *Journal* to publish its proceedings, and he was made editor, to act in consultation with the Publishing Committee of the council. Hind had entered a new world, much wider than that furnished by the Normal School. What was to be his true career had begun.

Hind also took in 1851 the step that was to separate him from the Normal School. While still a master at the school, he began to lecture in organic chemistry at the Medical Faculty of the University of Trinity College. The latter was the Church of England university Bishop John Strachan had established in 1850-1852 after King's College had been secularized as University College. The Medical Faculty had been started in 1850, as a private medical school, by Dr. E.M. Hodder and Dr. James Bovell as the Upper Canadian School of Medicine. In the same year it affiliated with Trinity College, and Hind's appointment as professor of chemistry followed in 1851.[13] In 1852 the Corporation of Trinity College required him to end his connection 'with any other institution,' and paid him a half-yearly salary of £75 for doing so.[14] In 1853 he was appointed to the faculty of Trinity College itself. The Corporation also, 'in consideration of the position the gentleman holds as Professor of the University,' made him a Master of Arts of Trinity, *jure dignitatis*, and at the same time made two medical instructors honorary Doctors of Medicine.[15]

The M.A., which appears so often behind Hind's name, was his solitary degree; it was no doubt more deserved academically than many honorary degrees given since, but it was honorary and not earned. The award is, however, illuminating. Trinity College, later to be rich and respected, was then new, small in faculty and student body, and poor. Such a college had to make academic bricks with what clay and straw could be assembled. For the circumstances, Hind was fairly well qualified. When he began his lectures in the autumn term of 1853, he had entered the portals of academic respectability. Moreover, having escaped the exacting demands of the Normal School, he was comparatively free to devote himself to his own interests and studies. How he was to fare was up to him. A Nottingham man could scarcely ask for more.

The best that can be said of Hind as instructor in chemistry and later in geology at Trinity is that his services must have been satisfactory. The outlines of his lectures are competent but not distinguished. Pertinent to the theme of his life is the heading of one lecture in geology: 'Distribution of Economic Material in Canada.'[16] Hind remained a member of Trinity College from 1853 to 1864, and then resigned of his own volition. There seems no reason to doubt that his professional knowledge of his two subjects was quite adequate for the instruction of undergraduates. His published essays make it evident that Hind possessed a gift for lucid and systematic exposition. His scientific writings suggest, to the layman, that he knew the language of both chemistry and geology. Trinity, moreover, as an Anglican college must have given him a congenial academic home. It must have been pleasant also to see the new buildings rise in their delightful situation on Queen Street, and Hind, a gardener, must have watched with pleasure as the new plantings took root and throve.

Anyone familiar with the spirit of such Anglican colleges might have questions about the professional spirit of their faculty, masters no doubt of language and idea but as craftsmen of culture rather than as keen, competitive scholars. One senses that the scientific spirit then came rather from University College than Trinity, and also that there may have been a certain polite enmity between Hind, with his rather casual training and his honorary M.A., and his colleagues at University College, Henry Holmes Croft and Edward John Chapman.[17] These men were professional scholars beyond doubt; in Logan's *Geology of Canada* (1863), for example, the reader senses his unspoken, but undoubtedly higher opinion of the geological work of Chapman than of Hind.[18] Hind had still to prove himself in his professed fields. The circumstances were, of course, not quite fair, for Hind taught in the two fields Croft and Chapman occupied singly. Hind, however, was not a man to be daunted by odds. It may be that the contact helped arouse the remarkable outburst of publications on scientific subjects and other writings which was to mark the years 1853-1864.

How likely such a possibility may be must be assessed from the story of those years. In the mid 1850s Hind was encouraged to think and publish on scientific subjects not, it may be supposed, by his teaching duties at Trinity, but by his connection with the Canadian Institute. That body not only gave him a circle of stimulating associates, one of whom, Sandford Fleming, was to prove a life-long friend, but also drew him into further lecturing and into editorial work. In these two activities Hind was to make a name sufficient to give him the opportunity from which his fame was to spring.

The *Canadian Journal*, the periodical founded by the institute and edited by Hind from 1852 to 1855, had a number of purposes, among them to publish the proceedings of the institute, and to encourage 'the Sciences and the Industrial Arts.' The latter purpose, which was taken seriously, arose both from the professional character of many of the founders, such as Fleming and Cumberland, and from the grant given by the provincial government to the institute on the understanding that its work would have utility in mind. The *Journal* could, of course, speak for itself. Despite its title and the recent national revolutions in Europe, 'We do not,' it declared in its opening editorial, 'appeal to the spirit of nationality...'

> We are endeavouring to supply such a publication as will afford a medium of communication between all engaged or interested in scientific or industrial pursuits, will assist, lighten and elevate the labours of the mechanic, will afford information to the manufacturer, and generally administer to the want [*sic*] of that already numerous and still increasing class in British America, who are desirous of becoming acquainted with the most recent inventions and improvements in the Arts and those scientific changes and discoveries which are in progress throughout the world.[19]

There is no need to think that Hind composed this weighty and Victorian sentence; it was perhaps the work of the Publishing Committee. Whoever the writer was, however, it stated the intentions of the institute clearly enough, and the *Journal* certainly attempted to carry out those purposes. A widening of scope even was to occur in the institute, and also in the periodical. As the *Journal* noted in its second volume, the institute was 'rapidly becoming the acknowledged centre of practical and theoretical science, as well as literature in Western Canada.'[20]

Together the institute and the *Journal* were, in fact, giving a forum and a voice to the small group of young and active professional and academic men who had come to Toronto in the 1840s, as Hind had done, and were eager to create in the rapidly growing town a focus of intellectual life that would serve at once their own careers and the community. 'Progress' was the keynote of the *Journal*; progress was the central part of their lives and of that of Toronto. The sense of advance was one aspect of, preceding, perhaps, but certainly incidental to, the telescoped growth of a town that was becoming the metropolis of Canada West.[21] The institute was at the same time a refuge for Upper Canadian conservatives, for men who had been excluded from political life by the rise of the new party politics, and who found the science and literature of Victorian Canada compatible with their social conservatism.[22] In such a group Hind, busy with his teaching, busy with his duties as editor of the *Journal* and in the council of the institute, was profitably at home. The conservative flavouring of the institute may well have been to his liking, even if unconsciously. He himself had no known political affiliation, but if anything he was by disposition conservative.

The chief evidences of his activities in the years from 1852 to 1857 are the first three annual volumes of the *Journal*, 1852-55, and five papers read before the institute. It cannot be said that Hind impressed his personality on the *Journal* as its editor. He was, perhaps, too young a man to do so, and was no doubt closely controlled by the Publishing Committee. The circumstances of his ceasing to be editor in 1855, to be replaced by Daniel Wilson of University College, are not known. No change of editorial tone is evident, but under the new editor a much improved, more scientific 'New Series' began. Hind's own writing for the *Journal* during his editorship cannot be identified, except in his signed papers and in the comments on the art exhibits at the Agricultural Exhibition of 1854. In those comments he spoke with the trenchancy that was his characteristic manner.[23] Of five papers and one commentary delivered before the institute, only one was published in the *Journal*.

This paper was his first for the institute, 'Notes on the Geology of Toronto,' read in January 1853 and published in the *Journal* the same year. It was also his first paper in geology, and reveals his already considerable skill as a descriptive geologist. The next year, 1854, saw his 'Report on the Preservation and Improvement of Toronto Harbour,' which was written in a public contest and for which he won a prize of £100. It was published as a supplement to the *Journal* in 1855. On 3 February 1855 he commented on a paper by Major R. Lachlan and General Cotton. In the discussion that followed, a friend recorded, Hind 'squabbled' with Chapman.[24] Hind himself on that date read a paper on a chemical subject, 'A Practical Introduction to a Mode of Manufacturing Gun Cotton.' On 24 February he followed with a paper 'On the North American Drift' and on 24 March one on 'The Origin of the Basin of the Great Lakes.'[25] They were more ambitious efforts, to judge by their titles, and they curiously suggest, perhaps accidentally, the geology of northwestern Canada and of lake formation with which he was soon to be occupied.

These last two papers, like that on the geology of Toronto, point to considerable field work – they could not have been works of the study only; but no more than one or two references to field work have survived. The three papers do indicate unmistakably, however, that Hind's scientific interests had come to centre in geology. And the geologist must go into the field, as members of the Geological Survey of Canada had been doing annually since its inception in 1842. The already famous and greatly respected head of that body, William Logan (soon to be Sir William), had read before the institute in the spring of 1854 a paper on 'The Physical Geography of Upper Canada,' a model of descriptive and analytical geological writing.[26] Hind would of course have met Logan, and his influence may have led Hind to devote himself to geology rather than chemistry.

Yet another pamphlet was prepared by Hind in these years, although it was not printed until 1857. This was his *Essay on the Insects and Diseases Injurious to Wheat Crops*, which he had written for a competition held by the provincial Department of Agriculture. Hind won 'first premium' and the reviewer of the pamphlet in the *Canadian Journal* noted that he had not used Killar's fundamental work on injurious insects.[27] For that Hind may have had some adequate reply, but for an understanding of his life the interest lies in his return to the subject of his first publication, the *Lectures*, and in another reminder that the 'Western Canada' of the 1850s was wheat country before all else. It also lies in the fact that a learned professor would enter the lists of such a competition.

It was no doubt the spirit of the decade that moved Hind to do so. The middle fifties saw a number of such essays, if perhaps less utilitarian, such as J.S. Hogan's on *Canada* and Alexander Morris's on *Canada and Her Resources*, both published in 1855. It was a decade of self-assessment, self-appreciation, and even downright boasting for western Canadians. It was also the decade of the Great Exhibition of 1851 and its successor at Paris in 1855, at which Canada won no fewer than 44 medals;

Hind was a member of the Toronto advisory committee to choose exhibits from Canada West.[28] Hind's serviceable brochure on agricultural pests by contrast seems modest.

More significant, however, was his beginning of straight commercial writing for the *Canadian Almanac*. The articles on 'The Future of Western Canada,' 1856, 'Our Railway Policy,' 1857, and finally 'The Great North-West,' 1858 (already written at the beginning of July 1857) reveal him as a student of the expansion of the Canadian frontier before he went to Red River. They no doubt earned him something.

Similar in character were two lectures given before the Mechanics' Institute of Toronto in January and February of 1857. One was on the possible use for 'The Manufacture of Illuminating Gas of the Utica Shales near Collingwood,' which Hind had examined in 1854. The second was on the 'Minerals of Canada'; in it Hind, taking up suggestions from Logan and T.S. Hunt, spoke of the prospects of mineral discoveries in the Laurentian rocks to the north. He stressed even more, from the same sources, the possibility of finding areas of 'crystalline limestone' in the Laurentian country, which would afford fertile land for agricultural settlement. Hind, the geologist, was thinking, as he was always to do, in terms of economic prospects, as a promoter as well as a scientist. No doubt he received some reward for these efforts, at least when they were published in the press.[29]

Hind was, it is evident, writing and lecturing for money. He had reason to do so, for he had become a victim of the raging prosperity of the mid 1850s, one of the great booms of Canadian history. Prices rose steadily but not, apparently, professors' stipends, at least not Hind's, in time to meet rising costs and the rapid increase of his family. The following episode is not in itself significant, but it is documented, a rare thing

in Hind's life, and it seems an indication of a
lack of means that was greatly to affect his life.

When the pinch became too great, Hind approached
Bishop Strachan as chairman of the Corporation of
Trinity College and requested an increase in salary.
The bishop entertained the request, for he wrote
to Hind on 23 October 1855 to say that a formal
application must be made through the bursar.
Strachan regretted that Hind had talked of his
interview with him, presumably among deeply interested colleagues. Such conduct the bishop thought
unusual among gentlemen, and destructive of confidence. Nevertheless, he would give the case
'favourable consideration so far as the state of
our funds will allow.'[30]

It was not altogether an auspicious opening but
Hind, no doubt because the need was great, set out
his request in writing.[31]

My Lord and Gentlemen,
I respectfully ask permission to submit to the
Council of Trinity College a request which is
urged upon me by circumstances over which I
have no control.
The very great rise in the price of provisions
and fuel, as well as in rents, during the past
year, has so seriously encroached upon the means
I possess of supporting my family, that I am
compelled by pressing necessity most respectfully
to solicit the attention of the Council to my
pecuniary position in relation to the College,
and if the circumstances of the case I offer
appear reasonable and just, to beg of the Council,
if it is in their power, to afford me a small
addition to my annual salary so that I may be
enabled to meet the unavoidable outlay which my
family requires.

         I have the honour to be ...
Rec'd and Read,   Henry Youle Hind,
19 Dec., 1855.   Prof. Chem.

It is a humble enough letter, and there is no reason not to think it genuine or that the facts are not as Hind stated. That being so, it is some evidence that Hind, besides the ambition of a bright boy from a well-to-do family fallen on hard times, and perhaps moved subconsciously to compensate for a rejection of his father's wish that he go into business, felt the insecurity of a largely self-trained scholar and scientist. Hind, at any rate, found himself with his young family in straitened circumstances. He might well begin to look for remuneration outside his salary and for additional employment; it is an old story in the profession of scholars. The Council's refusal or inability to increase Hind's stipend left him to face the situation as best he could.

Fortunately, an incident occurred in 1856 which pointed the way to a possible means of escape. In the summer of 1856 Hind accompanied Sandford Fleming on an expedition to the valley of the Saugeen river of Canada West to survey a railway line. It is the first record of Hind's experience of exploration in Canada. At the time perhaps it was little more than a pleasant summer outing, accompanied, one hopes, with some pay.[32] But it was exploration of a kind, it was to the westward, and it was a release from the genteel poverty of Trinity College. It was also an omen. For in 1856 a sudden interest had arisen among important people in Toronto, including George Brown of the *Globe*, in the northwest of British America.

III The Red River Expedition 1857

In 1856 the future of the northwest of British North America, territory held and governed, so far as it was governed, by the Hudson's Bay Company, was a growing interest in the province of Canada, and particularly in Toronto. The reasons were varied: a commercial appetite for a share in the fur trade now free of the monopoly of the Hudson's Bay Company – a new North West Company was talked of; an interest among farmers in new land – that of Upper Canada was nearly all taken up; a British interest in devolving upon Canada the near derelict régime of the Hudson's Bay Company; above all, the metropolitan ambitions of booming Toronto.[1] With all of these, except perhaps the British concern for the future of the Hudson's Bay territory, Hind must have been familiar. It is permissible to suppose that he, already writing for the *Canadian Almanac* on the Northwest, and Fleming, also interested in this region,[2] had discussed it in the evenings along the Saugeen in the summer of 1856.

Be that as it was, in the late fall of that year the Board of Trade in Toronto held hearings on the prospects of development in the Northwest, and early in 1857, in the session of the Canadian parliament in Toronto, pressure was put on the government of Etienne-Paschal Taché and John A. Macdonald to assert Canadian interests in the region. At the same time, the Hudson's Bay Company, only too aware that its future was in question, applied to the British government for a renewal of its licence to the exclusive trade of the Northwest, which was to expire in 1859.

The results were the same in both Canada and the United Kingdom: the appointment early in 1857 of a Select Committee of Enquiry both by the British House of Commons and by the Legislative Assembly of Canada. The British committee was weighty, and its inquiries were prolonged; it produced a report of some discernment and utility - one of its results was the creation of the colony of British Columbia. The other was very ordinary, and its work was superficial and patchy. The inquiries, however, led the respective governments to support exploring expeditions to the Northwest to prepare scientific reports on its material resources, its climate, and the prospects of the construction of a railway within British territory. The British government, in cooperation with Sir Roderick Murchison, distinguished geologist and president of the Royal Geographical Society, prepared the comparatively well-staffed and well-equipped expedition under Captain John Palliser. This party from 1857 to 1860 explored the Northwest from Lake Superior to the Pacific, much of it intensively by all past standards. In 1863 its large, complicated report appeared, which has only today received the analysis it deserved.[3] The Canadian government, possibly because of doubts on the part of its members from Canada East, was not so prompt, but by June 1857 it had decided to send an exploring expedition to the valleys of the Red and Saskatchewan rivers.[4] In this way came the opportunity which was to allow Hind to make his name.

For such an expedition he was, if a possible choice, certainly not an obvious one. There were, however, no obvious choices for an expedition of a kind novel in Canadian governmental experience, and political patronage, bestowed by responsible government on ministers of the Crown and members of the Assembly, was the established way of recruitment for government service. Hind therefore approached the Hon. Philip VanKoughnet, member of the Legislative Council and Minister of Agriculture in the Taché-Macdonald cabinet. He was as well a member of the Corporation of Trinity College and of its faculty of law. The Canadian government, however, like the British, had sought scientific advice on the appointment of experts as members of the expedition, and VanKoughnet referred Hind to Sir William Logan, director of the Geological Survey of Canada, whom, of course, Hind already knew through the Canadian Institute.

On 3 July 1857, therefore, Hind wrote to Sir William what is the fullest of his surviving letters, seeking support for his appointment as geologist and naturalist to the expedition.[5] He explained that his chief qualifications for the post consisted of having read the principal authorities on the northwest of the United States and British America, and in the preparation of his articles for the *Canadian Almanac*, 1856, 1857, and 1858. In addition he had lectured on geology at Trinity College for the past nine months; he enclosed his outline of lectures and the examination paper for Sir William's information. He had prefaced this qualification by stating that he by no means professed to be competent to interpret the geology of the country, but felt that he could observe the geological features and report what he saw.

Even more interesting than this revelation of what may be termed Hind's preparation for the exploration of the Northwest, and typical of his eager and thrusting temperament, was his submission, subject to Logan's own direction, of a plan of the route he thought the exploration should take. The explorers would go from Fort William to the Lake of the Woods, from there by the Roseau portage to Red River. From that point, they should proceed to the mouth of the Mouse (Souris) River, to examine the 'Grand Coulée' said to run from the Missouri to the Mouse and to investigate reported beds of lignite on the Souris as a possible source of fuel on the prairies. The return might be by Red River and St. Paul. (The plan was very much what Hind tried to do and largely did in 1857.) Finally, he assured Sir William, he was familiar with life on the prairies of Texas and Louisiana, and was capable of using both French and German. It was just such a letter as scholars write today in seeking a grant for research, even to the detail that he could if necessary easily get leave from Trinity College. Nothing could illustrate more clearly Hind's strong bent to explore the Northwest, with the hope, no doubt, of adding to his income.

Logan replied promptly in a cordial letter of 7 July.[6] The government had, he wrote, applied some time ago to him for a member of the staff of the Geological Survey to accompany the expedition. Everyone, however, was already in the field beyond reach of the mail, and the government had then asked for someone who might be capable of such a collection of facts and materials as would serve to indicate the main geological features of the country. Logan had suggested a person - no name is mentioned but it was probably the gifted amateur, James Richardson[7] - who had collected with ability and enthusiasm. He had heard nothing further on the subject.

He was fully persuaded, Logan went on, that Hind, if appointed, would make an excellent explorer and produce a valuable report. It would, therefore, give Logan much pleasure if there should be room for both the man he had recommended and Hind. Moreover, as it appeared Hind had some free time, would he have any objection to making an expedition in Canada for the Geological Survey if he should not go to the Northwest? If Hind were interested he should come to Montreal at Logan's expense.

The letter was, except for the fact of the previous recommendation, an undoubted approval of Hind for the post he coveted, and it may be assumed that it was the basis of his appointment. The letter is indeed the only known evidence of how Hind obtained the post, and in itself surely sufficient. It is, however, more than that. It reveals that at this date Logan, the towering summit of professional integrity and authority in Canadian geology, and greatly respected by geologists in Britain and the United States, had a good opinion of Hind as an apprentice geologist. He was even prepared to discuss using him in the work of the Survey itself, a service distinguished by an ascetic rigour and open only to those who passed the all-revealing search of Logan's eye. If Hind should confirm Logan's initial good opinion, either on the expedition or in a special assignment for the Survey, he might be able to establish himself in the profession of geological exploration, perhaps even enter the Survey itself, as Richardson was to do.

It was with such possibilities brightening the soft glow of Toronto's summer air that Hind began the great adventure of his life. For its sponsors the expedition of 1857 was to be mismanaged and in itself to prove of little value, but for Hind it was to be a chance to prove his quality as explorer and geological observer. It no doubt, therefore, did not greatly trouble him that the expedition began late because of the delay caused by the opposition to it. Not until 18 July was the minute of the Executive Council approving it passed. Preparations must have been going forward in anticipation of approval, as the party left Toronto five days later.

The expedition was a fair sample of the Canadian society which had launched it. The head was George Gladman, born in the Hudson's Bay Company territory and a former chief trader of the company until he retired to settle in Canada. He had been active in arousing the new interest in the Northwest, and had given evidence before the Canadian Select Committee earlier in 1857. Because of his experience, the veteran trader was put in charge of the expedition as a whole and made responsible for carrying out its 'primary object ... a thorough examination of the tract of country between Lake Superior and Red River.'[8] He, with his son Henry Gladman, his assistant, represented the old skills and interests of the fur trade. Associated with George Gladman, but with special instructions of their own, were Simon J. Dawson, civil engineer, and W.H.E. Napier, public land surveyor, with the joint responsibility for deciding how the old canoe route might be made a passage by road and water transport for settlers in the Northwest. Their assistants were S.L. Russell, G.F. Gaudet, A.M. Wells, J.A. Dickenson, and Robert Wynne, all representatives of the newer class of professional men who from the Eastern Townships of Canada East to Georgian Bay of Canada West were carrying the Canadian frontier forward by land road and railroad surveys. As levellers and chainmen, the engineers and surveyors had young men, like engineering students today, H.H. Killaly, Edward Cayley, J. Cayley, and another called Campbell, whose names gave rise to the *Globe*'s sour comment that the expedition was largely a summer outing for the sons of politicians. Included, perhaps for political reasons and for good

relations with the French element in Red River, was
Colonel Charles Irumberry de Salaberry, son of the
victor of Châteauguay. These were, in the language
of the day, 'the gentlemen' of the expedition.
With them were, as the man power of the party and
representatives of the fur trade, a dozen Iroquois,
and later the same number of Ojibwas and several
French Canadians, a half breed and a Scot.[9]

Hind himself was designated 'Geologist and Naturalist to the party' under the direction of Gladman.
He was to collect information for 'a description
of the main geological features of the country'
traversed, and to record 'whatever pertains to its
natural history' that he might have an opportunity
to observe. With reference to geology in particular
he was to be guided by the memorandum supplied by
Sir William Logan to the government and to give
special attention, as far as possible, to

> 1. The boundaries of formations. 2. The distribution of limestone. 3. The collection of fossils.
> 4. The occurrence of economic minerals. 5. The
> exact position of all facts, and the attitude of
> the rocks.

With respect to natural history, he was to collect
what he could and note as minutely as possible in
a daily journal 'all leading features of topography,
vegetation, and soil' along the line of route, as
well as make meteorological observations. Hind
was to be paid thirty shillings a day while on the
expedition - a princely rate compared with his
academic salary - and to have the appointment of
one assistant. He chose John Fleming, younger
brother of Sandford, another evidence of the friendly
relations between the elder Fleming and Hind. John
Fleming's particular duties were those of 'draughtsman,' and his pencil drawings and water colours
were to prove with Hind's writings among the lasting
results of the expedition.[10]

The historic Canada of the partnership of Indian and European and the new Canada of the engineer's and geologist's frontier were thus united in the hastily assembled party. On 23 July 1857 it entrained at the Toronto depot of the Northern Railway for Collingwood. The line, just completed in 1855, was itself an expression of the quest of Toronto for the trade of the upper lakes and the Northwest, and the work of engineers like Sandford Fleming and mining and railway promoters like Allan Macdonell.[11] The still humpy track winding to Barrie and to Collingwood on Georgian Bay had been laid for just such purposes as the party represented: migration, settlement, mining. The expedition, on reconnaissance for the Canadian frontier in the eager expansion of the fifties, was only a larger version of such expeditions as Sandford Fleming and Hind had made to the Saugeen in 1856, or Simon Dawson many times in the valleys of the Ottawa and St. Maurice rivers. Like them, it was to look, with the best scientific means available, for routes for road and railway, land for settlement, timber for felling, minerals for mining.

The *S.S. Collingwood*, a squat little paddlewheeler, left her home on 24 July with the party and its canoes brought from Lachine, and reached Sault Ste Marie on the 27th. It had bypassed the falls of St. Mary's River by the new American lock opened in 1855, on the significance of which for western expansion Hind was to dilate in his report. The ship entered at once into the storms and fogs of Lake Superior, to run aground that night on an island near Michipicoten harbour, as Fleming's sketch records.[12] When the *Collingwood* was refloated and repaired, the expedition resumed its voyage on 30 July, and the next day entered the grand portals of Thunder Bay. Here at Fort William the work of the expedition began, with the organization of two brigades of three canoes each, the hiring of twelve additional (Ojibwa) canoemen, and the sorting and packing of supplies.

Hind was free to occupy himself with observations of the region and to talk with Chief Trader John McIntyre of the Hudson's Bay Company post at Fort William and Father Jean-Pierre Choné of the Roman Catholic mission. As he had done since the party left Collingwood, he collected material for the journal on which he was to base his official report and ultimately his own *Narrative*. In doing so, he was, of course, following not only his instructions but also the discipline of all serious observers in the field. As surviving notebooks of Hind's in the Manitoba Archives in Winnipeg and in the Saint John Museum show, he was a regular and careful keeper of journals, and his work would always be based, whatever its ultimate form, on his own observations recorded on the spot. On this expedition these were amplified with thermometer readings of air and water temperatures, barometric readings of elevation, the results of the engineers' levellings, and similar scientific data. Hind was taking his duties with the utmost seriousness, the seriousness of a man who had found his calling. It is to be noted also how amply he interpreted his already broad instructions; he would be equipped to write a report of the whole expedition, and even more than a report.

On 3 August, the first brigade, under Dawson and Hind, started up the Kaministiquia River for the long haul over the height of land to Rainy River. Wynne was left at Fort William to lay out a road from Thunder Bay to the river above the great Kakabeka Falls, the beginning of what was later to be known as the 'Dawson route.'[13] The second brigade, led by Gladman, overtook the first on 5 August. From then on the brigades travelled together, except that Gladman in a single canoe from 9 August pushed on a day ahead for Fort Frances to secure canoemen in place of the Fort William Indians

for the rest of the journey to Red River.[14] Hind
found he had little opportunity or means to observe
or to scout away from the line of the canoe route.[15]
It is probable that in this forced pace there began
those personal frictions that were to affect the
expedition's outcome. The route, of course, was
well known, not only to Sir George Simpson and his
company's fur traders, but also to scientists.
Alexander Murray of the Geological Survey had followed it as far as the height of land in 1847, Sir
John Richardson had used it only nine years before
in 1848, and Palliser a mere month before.[16] Hind
was crossing country also relatively well known
geologically, and only the special economic concerns of the Red River Expedition made further
investigation desirable. Not until Red River was
reached would he be able to hope for fresh areas
to observe.

At Fort Frances, reached on 19 August, the party
was well received by Postmaster Robert Pether of
the Hudson's Bay Company, and paused to prepare
the advance to Red River and to report progress to
Toronto. It was decided to divide the expedition
into three parties. One under Napier would follow
a canoe route east of the Lake of the Woods from
Fort Frances to the Winnipeg River to learn whether
it might be a useful line of passage.[17] The main
party under Gladman would push on by the traditional
way by Rat Portage (Kenora) to Red River to make
preparations for further exploration there. John
Fleming went with this party to make observations
for Hind, and according to his later account it
travelled in fur trade fashion, over-loaded and
under-provisioned.[18] The third party, headed by
Dawson and Hind, with only two canoes and six men
in all (including Lambert, the French Canadian),
was, against Gladman's wishes, to cross the southern
body of the Lake of the Woods, to portage by the
marshes of the west shore to the Roseau River, and

to go down it to the Red. This exploration was
what Hind had proposed to Logan and the purpose
was clearly to see a part of the country different
in kind as well as location from the area of the
Winnipeg River. Pether warned the two men that
Palliser's party had made the Indians uneasy, and
that a war party of Ojibwa would be returning from
a raid on the Sioux of the plains by the route
Hind and Dawson had chosen. It was an ominous
note.[19]

On Saturday, 22 August, Hind and Dawson set out
from Fort Frances down the broad Rainy River to
the Lake of the Woods.[20] Hind, like all travellers
before him, noted the belt of land on either side
of the river suitable for agriculture. He noted
also the Indian graves and great mounds, relics
of the aboriginal way of life that still continued
along their line of advance. Next day they entered
the great southeastern bay of the lake, and set out
across the calm, warm waters for Keating Island,
dim and blue to the northwest. The water was full
of 'the weed,' algae breeding in the August heat,
and increasingly spotted with floating grasshoppers
from the huge swarms coming in from the plains to
the southwest.[21] Their goal that day was Garden
Island which lay out in the southwest bay of the
lake, into which the Muskeg River flowed from the
west; by it they planned to make their way to the
headwaters of the Roseau. By evening they reached
the northwest corner of the island, in the teeth
of a rising gale. Garden Island was so called
because the Ojibwas since the last century had
used it to grow corn, potatoes, pumpkin, and squash
where there were no deer to destroy their plots,
unattended during the summer's fishing and berry-
picking. Hind collected samples of the corn growing
there and noted the ravages of the swarming locusts
and the incessant grinding of their multitudinous
jaws.

That evening, by the camp fire, Dawson and the
Iroquois voyageur, Pierre, both complained of being
unwell. The fire attracted the attention of the
Ojibwa raiding party Pether had spoken of, camped
on Massacre Island, four miles off across the restless water. The travellers were wakened at midnight
by two emissaries from them. These nocturnal mes-
sengers insisted that a council be held next day
with the chiefs and men of the region. Next morning
a flotilla of 13 canoes descended on Garden Island
with 53 men, some of them still wearing the war
paint and feathers of the raid from which they were
returning. Hind and Dawson found themselves facing
an assembly of respectful and deferential, but
quietly determined Indians. The two men had hastily
conferred and it was agreed that Hind would take
notes while Dawson talked, through one of their men
as interpreter, with the chief spokesman, an aged
man happily not in war paint. Thus it happened
that there exists a full record of the council
between the guardians of the ancient Indian life
and the pioneers of the new.[22]

As so often in such a conference, the representatives of 'civilization' had decided to be evasive
with the 'wild' men. The Indians simply wanted to
know why Hind and Dawson wished to go to Red River
by the Roseau rather than by the traditional way
of the Winnipeg. As Hind had been warned at Fort
Frances, their suspicions had been aroused by the
activity of the botanist of Palliser's party,
Eugène Bourgeaux, in collecting plants. They had
assumed, quite rightly, that this betokened an
interest in the land for settlement, and now here
was Hind, as they gravely pointed out, collecting
corn on Garden Island. Had he not seen corn before,
came the quiet ironic question? Dawson stalled; he
would only say that he and Hind were proceeding
under orders they must obey, a statement not altogether true in the light of Gladman's objection to

their plan. As a result, Dawson quite failed to
allay, and probably only confirmed, the Indians'
suspicions. So they made their decision, politely
but firmly. They would not furnish guides for the
difficult route, unknown to Hind and Dawson. They
could not, declared the old chief, allow the white
men to go on by any route but that by the Winnipeg.
'It is hard,' he said in a passage Hind had the
grace to quote in his *Narrative*,

> to deny your request; but we see how the Indians
> are treated far away. The white man comes, looks
> at their flowers, their trees, and their rivers;
> others soon follow; the lands of the Indians pass
> from their hands, and they have nowhere a home.
> You must go by the way the white man has hitherto
> gone. I have told you all.

Before this finality Dawson and Hind were helpless. The Indian guide Gladman had obtained for
them at Fort Frances had not come because he had
fallen sick. (Was his sickness diplomatic, or was
it real and the origin of Dawson's and Pierre's
mounting fever?) With no guide and two sick men,
it was impossible to plunge into the marshes on
the flat height of land between the Muskeg and the
Roseau. Even to go by the Winnipeg they would need
help. They gave up their purpose, therefore, and
the council ended in great friendliness. The old
chief explained his firmness:

> We have hearts, and love our lives and our country.
> If twenty men came we would not let them pass to-
> day. We do not want the white man; when the white
> man comes, he brings disease and sickness, and our
> people perish... Many white men would bring death
> to us, and our people would pass away; we wish to
> love and to hold the land our fathers won, and the
> Great Spirit has given to us.

But he and his warriors were prepared to be
friendly, even in the face of this insidious danger,
and when Dawson confessed at last that they had intended to go by the Muskeg-Roseau portage to see
whether Americans were using it, the council ended
amicably. It was a sobering lesson for Hind, which
he did not forget, and one of the virtues of the
Narrative he was to write was to be its feeling for
the plight of the Indians before the frontier Hind
was pushing forward. Dawson was to warn the Canadian
government it must make a treaty with the Indians
of Rainy River and Lake of the Woods, who could yet
muster 800 warriors.[23] His warning was to be remembered by the government a decade later, when,
still with no treaty made, it had to think of sending
a military expedition to a Red River in revolt.

For the present, however, the friendliness of
the mollified Indians was genuine. Two young men
were told to go with Dawson and Hind, one as far
as Islington Mission on the Winnipeg River, one as
far as Red River itself. It was indispensable aid,
for already Pierre was helpless, and by morning
Dawson too could only lie limp in the bottom of
his canoe. During four days, except for one pounding
hailstorm, Hind threaded the Lake of the Woods and
then began to follow the current of the Winnipeg
through its narrows and lakes. He administered
what medicine he had for fever to the sick men,
and still observed the wild and beautiful country
of the region. On Saturday, 28 August, the party
reached Islington Mission at the White Dog falls
of the Winnipeg, where the Rev. Robert McDonald,
half-breed Church of England priest, was in charge.[24]

The site of the mission, first begun and then
abandoned by the Roman Catholic priest George-
Antoine Bellecourt, and founded again by the Anglicans
in 1852, was a small area of good soil set just above
the river. There grain and vegetables were being
raised for food, in the hope of converting the

Swampy Cree hunters of the region north of the
Winnipeg to some part-time agriculture. Here the
sick men could at least be rested. Pierre, breaking
out in blotches, passed the crisis of the disease,
and began to recover. But Dawson became even worse,
lapsing at one point into delirium and having in
fact a severe case of typhus. Hind and McDonald
thought Hind should continue in order to try to
overtake the main party, but Dawson would not hear
of Hind's going.[25]

Hind, therefore, waited over Sunday. On Monday,
with McDonald's support, he set out for Red River,
leaving Dawson once more lucid enough to write
notes to Gladman and Wells, but, as events were to
prove, really no better. All that week Hind's
canoe drove rapidly down the river, only to be held
up by stormy weather on the shallow and dangerous
southern end of Lake Winnipeg. The night of Friday,
4 September, was spent in the canoe in the reeds
awash with waves from the lake. But the next day
Hind passed through the delta of the Red and ascended to where the main party was encamped near
Upper Fort Garry.[25]

All the way Hind had continued his observations,
but with constant thought for the helpless Dawson.
Disappointed in not finding medical help at Fort
Alexander at the mouth of the Winnipeg, he now
sought Gladman at Fort Garry to have him order a
canoe to return to Islington with medicines and
food for Dawson. Then the smouldering friction
that had disturbed the expedition burst into open
flame. Gladman's men at Fort Garry were unhappy.
Left on their own, as they thought, by the old fur
trader, who had gone on ahead of them at Big Dog
portage above Fort Frances, and hard driven from
Fort Frances to Lower Fort Garry, they had arrived
there only to see Gladman leave them to go to stay
with his daughter. He refused for them the invitation of A.R. Lillie, the officer in charge of the

lower fort, to stay in its large, well-furnished
quarters, saying, 'the gentlemen would be happy in
their tents.' The party had, therefore, to paddle
some 25 miles to the upper fort, and there pitch
tent for their stay. They encamped, unknowingly,
on a public thoroughfare, perhaps the equivalent
of the present south Main Street of Winnipeg, and,
finding themselves without wood, helped themselves
to the supply of the Hudson's Bay Company. To both
the error in the campsite and the purloining of the
wood, Chief Factor William Mactavish of Upper Fort
Garry objected stiffly, if politely.[27]

Hind thus joined a weary and disgruntled band of
Canadians, all too aware that they were strangers
in a strange land and hard set to obtain supplies
then and later because of the demands of a detach-
ment of the Canadian Rifles come to garrison the
colony. Hind found too that he had passed Gladman
comfortably resting down the river among friends
and relatives in St. Andrew's parish. Wells, although Dawson's assistant, would not assume responsibility for sending off a canoe at once, nor
would Hind, perhaps in both instances because they
had not met with a doctor. Gladman had, therefore, to be found, as he was by Wells the next day,
Sunday 6 September, after some difficulty. He
declared it impossible to man and equip a canoe on
Sunday, and Dr. John Bunn, when consulted in his
office at the upper fort, was reluctant to prescribe
for a case he had not diagnosed. Moreover, it took
all Monday and the early morning of Tuesday to prepare and send off a canoe under Gaudet for the relief of Dawson.[28]

In Gladman's defence, it is necessary to note
that it was Sunday before he could take charge,
that Red River people were notoriously slow starters,
that the men of the survey party were weary, that
perhaps nothing could have been done more quickly.
Happily, Dawson did not suffer for the time lost.

He had indeed almost died after Hind's departure; so desperate did his condition become that McDonald, perhaps stirred by some atavistic faith, called in an Indian medicine man - the region was, as it is still, noted for its medicine men and the making of medicine. After he had 'administered the specifics' to the sick man his recovery began. When Gaudet's canoe arrived with supplies, Dawson's convalescence was continuing, and he was able to reach Red River on 8 October.[29]

The dissatisfaction with Gladman's leadership, however, had pretty well broken up the party. Hind wrote to the Provincial Secretary, Timothy Lee Terrill, on 9 September to say there were grave causes of irritation with the conduct of the expedition which might 'prove very disastrous' to many of its objects. He would, however, say nothing until he got back to Toronto, but would do so then if invited.[30] In Red River Gladman's leadership was at an end. (Although he was reticent in the letter Hind had alleged in it that the expedition had elected its own leader en route, whom he does not name.) Gladman busied himself, aided by de Salaberry, with the provision of supplies and horses for the various parties into which the expedition now separated, and with arrangements for the explorations of 1858. The engineers Wells and Dickenson, as instructed by Dawson in his hasty note from Islington, began to explore the country eastward towards the Lake of the Woods for a land road that would avoid the many falls of the Winnipeg. Hind, who had obtained a house for his party in the Middle Settlement, was free to undertake his observations of the main features and agricultural possibilities of the Red River valley.[31]

Now in effect on his own, Hind had three things to do to complete his commission for 1857. One was to explore Red River settlement itself. The second was to examine the Assiniboine westward as far as Portage la Prairie and make inquiries about the lignite coal of the Souris valley. The third was to explore the Red River valley southward to the Roseau and examine that river sufficiently to understand the nature of the route from the Lake of the Woods, which the Indians at Garden Island had prevented him from using. He had, as it turned out, a full month for his tasks from 9 September to 8 October.

As the Red River Settlement lay exclusively along the river fronts of the Red and Assiniboine, Hind had already seen a great part of it on his trip up the Red from the delta to the Forks on 6 September. He would learn much about it in outfitting for the trip to Portage on 9 and 10 September, because he dealt with Andrew McDermot, the well-known private trader of Red River. The Canadian government gave its business to McDermot rather than to the Hudson's Bay Company, which may have added to Mactavish's frigidity over the stolen firewood, for normally hospitality in Red River was lavish, even if wood was a scarce article by 1857. Hind was also in the settlement after his return from Portage on 16 September until his departure for the Roseau on the 21st. From the Roseau he returned to the settlement again on 29 September, which left him a week in hand before he had to prepare to leave for Toronto. He spent it going over Red River from the Indian Mission towards the delta to the French settlements above the Forks. Hind also talked with many Red River people, from McDermot, who had been in the settlement since 1823, to Donald Gunn, a self-trained scientist and already a correspondent of the Smithsonian Institution. Unfortunately, the historian of Red River, Alexander Ross, had died in 1856. Among those Hind met were some of the missionaries, Anglican and Roman Catholic, and the one Presbyterian, the Rev. John Black. No doubt he conferred with other farmers than those he tells of at length in the *Narrative*. Although he does not mention doing so it is probable he discussed the colony with Hudson's Bay Company officers, for Hind had none of the Canadian prejudices against the company and later was careful to speak well of it and express his gratitude for the help its officers had given him. As a result of his observation and investigation, he became well informed about the agricultural potentialities of Red River, the nature and condition of the colony, and the character and disposition of its two communities, English and French by language if in the larger part of mixed blood. He thus spent his time in the Red River Settlement to best advantage and his description of it was to be perhaps the best ever made of that picturesque, slovenly community so delicately balanced between the primitive and the civilized.

The trip to Portage la Prairie, made with Napier, gave him a similar if more superficial view of the country of the western settlements along the Assiniboine from St. James' parish by Lane's Post to Portage itself. Hind turned slightly aside midway on his trip to examine the Big Ridge north of the Assiniboine and he quickly grasped the nature of that limestone plateau, a feature which was to reappear in his observations in 1858. At Portage itself, Hind began inquiries about the lignite of the Souris, and had the report confirmed by John Spence, a leading settler of Portage, and a provident farmer who gave Hind his first information on the Indian corn of Red River, the so-called 'Mandril,' or, as Hind rightly conjectured, Mandan corn. He attempted to organize an expedition to the Souris but lack of time made it impossible for him to get together a large enough party, in view of a successful theft of horses by a party of Sioux from the buffalo hunters' caravan only half a day's journey southwest of Portage. In this incident Hind made his first acquaintance with the caution about the

'Plains' tribes that conditioned all movement beyond the line of the parkbelt country.

He therefore turned back, and in the settlements along the Assiniboine in St. Margaret's parish (Headingley) had the two interviews with Red River farmers the second of which is perhaps the best known passage in his *Narrative*. One was with George Flett, who confirmed what Spence had said about Indian corn, that it would ripen in favourable locations and seasons, and who first gave Hind the message that was to ring loudest among the farmers of Ontario, that thirty bushels an acre of wheat might be expected on older land and forty bushels on new. It was, however, on the farm of Oliver Gowler, 'nine miles from Fort Garry,' that Hind witnessed both the possibilities and the frustration of Red River agriculture. Gowler was a Lincolnshire farmer brought out by the company in 1836 to help run its second experimental farm. That had failed, and Gowler had then set up for himself. He was cultivating fifty acres with abundant returns, but touched no more of his extensive farm for want of markets. He had proved, as Hind's account makes clear, that good farming would be richly rewarded in the standard grains, in vegetables, and in livestock, but would choke in its own abundance for want of a local market or a railway to wider markets.

Hind, neither in his formal 'Report' nor in the *Narrative*, could leave the matter at that. He gave a lively account of an incident which occurred when Gowler took his guests in to dinner. Mrs. Gowler, good English farmer's wife that she was, had been mindful of the Old Country distinction between gentlemen and farmers, and had set no plate for Gowler, much less for herself. Puzzled, he asked,

'And where is my plate?' 'Oh, John [Oliver]! you would not think of sitting at table with gentlemen?' Mr. John seemed puzzled for a moment; his son-in-law and children were looking in silence from different corners of the room. He cast a hasty glance around, and the true feelings of independence and manly right showed themselves, as he exclaimed, 'Give me a chair and a plate; am I not a gentleman, too? Is not this my house, my farm, and these my victuals? Give me a plate.'

It is the first recording of the voice of western agrarian democracy, and Hind caught it fully.

He had caught not less fully the spirit of the Canadian expedition, which was to make clear whether the frontier of 'Western Canada' was to continue to flow, as to a great degree it then did, into the American midwest, or to find an alternative in the northwest above and beyond the lakes. For the Canada of the St. Lawrence, like the United States, might be made a great nation by the west. The expedition was indeed a reconnaisance to discover whether Canada had its own, authentic future, or whether it was, largely because of the French occupation of the lower St. Lawrence, only an unfortunate departure, like the south of the United States, from the American pattern, forged in New England and elaborated in the middle colonies and the midwest.

On a mission so important, there could be no easy, lazy delay. The drive of industrial Nottingham, the urgencies of the Stoney Gate, were at work. On 21 September Hind set out with John Fleming from Fort Garry southward by the west bank of the Red River for Pembina. Pembina had been a settlement of Red River Métis on the west bank of the Red but on the American side of the 'lines,' the 49th parallel, and by its position it had served as a base for Métis opposition to the monopoly of trade held by the Hudson's Bay Company under the licence of 1839. When the coming of 'free trade' after 1849 had made opposition unnecessary and the flood of 1852 had proved the site undesirable, the Métis had abandoned it for St. Boniface or for St. Joseph's below the Pembina escarpment to the west. Thereafter open trade between Red River and St. Paul by Red River cart brigade had made Pembina no more than a stopping place. Hind followed the cart trail to Pembina, was entertained by the Hudson's Bay Company officer north of the 'lines,' crossed the Red, and ascended the Roseau.

Although he does not say so, it is apparent that he discovered the Roseau route from the Lake of the Woods to the Red was no more than it had been in the days of Dufrost de La Jemerais in 1734, a route a resolute man who did not mind being wet to the waist for two or three days might use. But it was one no party of immigrants could use, and certainly no American in his right mind would, if any ever had, as Dawson had suggested to the Indians of Garden Island.

What Hind did discover, and ably described, was the lake beach east of Red River, which divided the relatively well-drained and highly fertile lands of the Red River valley from the poorly drained lands to the eastward. He rightly saw in it a natural line of travel from the Red River Settlement to the south, as in fact it was to become. But was Hind, in this concern for ways of travel, not transgressing on the preserves of Dawson and his engineers? In the enthusiasm of the expedition of 1857, the question is no doubt a niggling one. The matter behind the question, however, was to have serious consequences, not only for the Canadian explorations but also for the career of Hind himself.

In the September weather of the prairies, as poplar and birch were turning gold against the dark green of spruce and jack pine, there was no time for such thoughts. Hind and Fleming, having probed the course of the Roseau up to the sullen and solitary marshes of the height of land plateau between the Red and the Lake of the Woods, turned north back to the settlement. Again the incessant observations are recorded; again the vast simplicity of the west, where the brush-strokes of creation are broad and sweeping, unlike the Hobbema delicacy of the east, is made evident as in no writer before Hind and by no draughtsman before Fleming.[32] Again there is an interview with a thriving Red River farmer, this time a Frenchman, Pierre Gladieux, as though Hind had possessed the calculated tact of a member of a royal commission on biculturalism. Gladieux represented as well as Flett or Gowler, for his part of the population, what industry, intelligence, and thrift could do with the resources of Red River within the limits of its narrow market.

What Hind was saying, in his reports of the experience of Gowler and Gladieux, although, as was his wont, he did not say it explicitly - he was a reporter of impressions rather than an analyst of evidence - was that an energetic and a careful man might live well in a simple way in Red River. If he were not both energetic and careful, he would have to turn to the two 'natural' occupations of Red River, the buffalo hunt and the illicit trade in furs. To these in fact the native people of Red River - neither Gowler nor Gladieux was a native - had increasingly turned. With the propensity to hunt rather than farm Hind, too, was to deal, but in the rush of the last days in Red River the full significance of his observations did not come through to him.

By 29 September he was once more back in the Middle Settlement. From there he made his final survey and investigation of the peculiar Red River community. In it the primitive wilderness and men skilled in wilderness crafts joined with a hierarchical and remote world of big business, itself conducted on the spot by plain Orkney and Scots men. These, in yet another involution, had risen, as had the great Sir George Simpson, from origins little more sophisticated than those of the buffalo-hunters. Hind's final survey too was hasty, but, as all his later work was to prove, a fine example of the art of the researcher whose grant is running out.

Hind did, however, delay his departure until S. J. Dawson, now recovered, arrived from Islington on 8 October. He had stayed to assure himself, as was only humane, of Dawson's welfare, for Dawson was to remain in Red River over winter, with 'excellent accommodation within half a mile from Fort Garry.'[33] But it may also be supposed that the two men at the time were closely united against Gladman. He, they felt, had made the expedition a farce and endangered the lives of its members; if there was any justification for this hurried, ill-organized journey, it was their own work. In their feelings lay the outcome of the expedition of 1857 and the character of that of 1858.

The ventilation of those grievances and difficulties awaited Hind's return to Toronto. Gladman had returned there by canoe early in September. Napier, Russell, Wells, Gaudet, with some of the chainmen, remained in Red River with Dawson, to survey the land route to the Lake of the Woods. Fleming, Dickenson, and Edward Cayley set out ahead of Hind by the trail to St. Paul,[34] and were overtaken by him on 9 October. During the same day the party met Bishop David Anderson of Rupert's Land, returning with his sister from England. His absence had, of course, deprived Hind of one important source of information on Red River where Anderson had been since his installation in 1849. From Pembina the party passed rapidly by the eastern, or 'wood,' trail to Crow Wing, which they reached on 24 October. The indefatigable Hind, revealing that his intentions extended beyond a mere report of his observations within British territory, kept the same careful, descriptive record of what he saw as the carts creaked and the horses plodded southward. From St. Cloud they went by stage coach to St. Paul, by steamboat to Prairie du Chien, and from there by rail to Toronto, which they reached on 4 November.

The explorers were home from the prairies, but the work of the expedition was by no means over, especially for the enthusiastic and ambitious Hind, who had found the occupation to which he could give everything he had. A report had to be prepared, and an expedition to the Saskatchewan organized. Hind had written from St. Paul to the Provincial Secretary, Terrill, and asked that he be allowed four months from his arrival in Toronto to write his report. He needed time, he said, to consider material noted in his daily journals 'for further study or reference.' Part of the letter was an outline for the report.[36]

He had therefore to spend the winter of 1857-1858 writing and seeing printed his report of the expedition of 1857, as well as teaching at Trinity and taking up new duties as curator of the Royal Canadian Institute.[37] The report, dated February 1858, was printed in haste, as somewhat numerous omissions and errors in detail indicate. It ran to over 400 pages, and was much more than a summary of Hind's own observations and journal. Scientific in form and wholly impersonal, it was, in fact, a report for the whole expedition, as though Hind had been leader and director. In addition, it was supplemented lavishly with tables, not all of which Hind had prepared himself, and was filled out with quotations, sometimes many pages long, from the

published work of other scientists and authors.
The most notable of the quotations, perhaps, is
one two pages in length, from Lorin Blodget's
Climatology of the United States, giving Blodget's
view of the significance of the northwestward
trend of the summer isothermal lines. It is
thrown in with obvious haste, without digestion
by Hind or correlation with his own observations.[38]
It is used simply to support Hind's general con-
tention that the valleys of the Red and the
Saskatchewan were suitable for agricultural settlement while the American far west was not.
The explorer and scientific observer had all too
clearly become the publicist and the promoter.
The comment of William Macdonell Dawson, Simon's
brother and in the Department of Crown Lands, was,
therefore, much to the point. Hind's work was,
he wrote to Simon, 'quite a Book - not properly
forming part of his report - which [as a whole]
is in fact more a compilation than a report.'
The legislature's Committee on Printing had required that everything Hind submitted should be
printed because the desire for information on
the Northwest was, Dawson went on, 'so general
and intense' it was bound to be wanted. As Hind,
Dawson concluded, 'is a pretty good writer, it
should be very interesting.'[39] William Dawson's
restrained approval of, it is presumed, Hind's
manuscript report is of interest. As the events
of the next year were to reveal, S.J. Dawson and
Hind were rivals in finding the best route to the
far west and British Columbia. Simon Dawson had
the considerable advantage of a brother who was
both a civil servant and in touch with men ambitious to organize a route to the Northwest. The
exploration of 1857 was by no means a mere academic
exercise.

    Hind's report was well received by the press,
especially the *Globe*. The reception justified

the expedition of 1857 and ensured that of 1858. Quite apart from the publicity and the reputation won for the author, Hind himself had come out of the hasty and ill-managed exploration well. William Dawson, in a memorandum to T.J. Loranger, the Provincial Secretary, written presumably at the latter's request, wrote of Hind on the 1857 expedition, 'I believe he was well qualified for the duties assigned to him. His reports speak for themselves.'[40] In fact only Hind and Simon Dawson were deserving of credit from the expedition. Simon Dawson wrote in April 1858 to his brother that anything accomplished for 'an enormous cost and unnecessary expense' had been accomplished by his party. Others, 'if I except Professor Hind,' had done nothing.[41] But even Gladman had taken occasion in January 1858 to assure Loranger that he was not antagonistic to 'the Professor' and suggest that Hind should be appointed geologist to the expedition of 1858 to explore the iron and salt deposits referred to in the evidence given the British Select Committee of 1857.[42]

Loranger initially proceeded to organize the 1858 expedition along the lines of that of 1857, and even sent Gladman instructions to prepare to lead it.[43] But thereupon the discontent with Gladman's leadership was voiced by Hind and Simon Dawson. The complaints of Hind after Dawson's illness had not appeared in his report, of course, nor were the letters of grievance published with it. But the dissatisfaction of Dawson and Hind with Gladman's leadership was known in the government and could not be ignored when the second expedition was being prepared. The task of stating fully the complaint against Gladman largely fell to Hind in Simon Dawson's absence in Red River. After collecting opinions from Fleming and Dickenson, Hind set out his grounds of dissatisfaction in full and in order in a letter to Loranger on 31 March

1858. They were, first, that although Hind's instructions had authorized him to leave the expedition when his work required, Gladman had refused to obtain the light canoe that would enable him to do so. Second, from the Big Dog portage, Gladman had gone on ahead of the expedition, making it impossible to see him; the rest of the party had to make out as best they might without his experience. Third, he had opposed the plan of Dawson and Hind to proceed by the Roseau to Red River. Fourth, Gladman had remained at the Lower Fort from 6 to 9 September, leaving the expedition without food or wood and hence in difficulties with Mactavish. Fifth, he had refused the invitation of 'Mr. Lily [*sic*],' the officer in charge of the Lower Fort, to have the expedition stay there. Sixth, his conduct had been criticized by many of the principal people at Red River. Seventh, against Hind's wishes, he had forced Lambert, the French Canadian voyageur and cook, to return to Canada with him, when Hind was to have had his services in Red River. Finally he was responsible for the delay in getting food and medicine to Dawson at Islington.[44]

Gladman, to judge by his letters to Loranger, behaved well when Hind's points were conveyed to him, with a copy of Hind's letter to the Rev. Robert McDonald at Islington setting out Hind's difficulties in getting help for Dawson. He defended his actions in moderate terms, even the delay in getting relief to Dawson, and betrayed no animosity towards those he must have known were his critics. One is left with a certain admiration for the old trader. His main defence, and it is borne out by William Dawson's memo on the expedition, was that he could not be held wholly responsible, for he was in fact not wholly in charge. Because there were three sets of instructions, there had been not one party but three, and therefore not one leader but three. Even so, taking the loose organization of the expedition into account, a distinct impression remains that Gladman took his responsibilities, however limited, too lightly, and in fact not only did little for the expedition but did that little rather badly. He was, perhaps, too much the old fur trader, accustomed to drive his men and make do with short supplies.[45]

At any rate, it was clear he could be dispensed with, and he was. He faded gracefully out of the picture.[46] That left Hind and Dawson, and in 1858 each was put in command of his own expedition. Hind was now independent, with the wide Assiniboine and Saskatchewan before him for the great expedition of 1858. He had earned the commission; but the student of his life must note that he had overthrown his leader to do so, as he had, it seems, challenged the headship of Robertson at the Normal School. And had he appropriated other men's work too readily in his ambitious report?

IV The Assiniboine and Saskatchewan Expedition 1858-1860

The Red River expedition of 1857 was at best a hasty reconnaisance, productive of little, despite Hind's *Report*, either in scientific knowledge or in practical information. The Canadian government, nevertheless, did not consider giving up its own exploration of the Northwest. It decided, when it learned how things had really gone, to avoid the confusion in the organization of the expedition of 1857 by dispensing with a general leader and by imposing financial controls. In 1858 there were to be two expeditions, each under its own leader with his own instructions. A record was to be kept of each for audit. One expedition, under S.J. Dawson, was to survey the country from Red River to Fort William for an immigrant route. The other, under Hind himself at $6.00 a day, exploring westward from Red River to the south branch of the Saskatchewan River, was to examine the suitability of the territory for settlement and in particular the lignite of the Souris valley and the salt springs of Lake Winnipegosis. The plan was clear and simple, and none of the mismanagement or bickering of 1857 was to occur in the expedition of 1858.[1]

Hind was indeed alert and meticulous in the preparation of his expedition, which was to be the main achievement of his life. Not only was he careful, when the time came, to print his instructions at the head of his report; he was careful to adhere to them in the field and in writing his report, with one exception. He had in fact suggested what the instructions should contain, especially the injunction to survey the lignite of the Souris and the salt springs of Winnipegosis.[2] He busied himself with the organization, going to Montreal to call on Sir George Simpson at Lachine and obtain introductions to Hudson's Bay Company officials, and to engage Iroquois canoemen from Caughnawaga. (He was to boast he had got the best of them.)[3]

Moreover, he persuaded the government to allow him to make an addition to his party, which suggests he may already have been looking beyond the expedition and his report to wider publication. The addition was Humphrey Lloyd Hime, whom Hind described as 'a practical photographer of the firm of Armstrong, Hime and Bare, Toronto. In addition to the qualification of being an excellent photographer he is also a practical surveyor.' He would 'furnish a series of collodion negatives of all objects of interest.'[4] Hime indeed proved to be a very good cameraman. Surviving photographs show that he caught the expanse of the prairies, the detail of life on the trail, the muddy slovenliness of the Red River Settlement. His pictures were to be the basis of the coloured lithographs of Hind's *Narrative* of the Assiniboine and Saskatchewan expedition in due course. The appointment of Hime reveals Hind's keen interest in publicity as does his requesting permission in April for the editor of the *Illustrated London News*, then 'in this city,' to reproduce sketches of the expedition of 1858. For his party Hind also chose his now veteran associates and supporters of 1857, J.A. Dickenson and John Fleming. These with Hind and Hime were the 'gentlemen' of the party; the men were the thirteen Iroquois, whose names Hind was to list in the *Narrative*, to whom an Ojibwa and two French Canadians were added later.[5]

In one other respect Hind was determined to improve on the performance of 1857. An early start was necessary, partly to furnish Dawson with the money, men, and supplies Hind was charged to take to him so that he might begin his survey eastward in good time, partly to make an early start westward possible for himself. This consideration had prompted the obtaining of the crack Iroquois canoemen, who would of course turn back at Red River. The feeling cannot be escaped that Hind was keen to outdo his competitors in the strenuous field of canoe travel: the great Sir George Simpson, whom he did outdo, and perhaps the stern field geologists of the Geological Survey. His party left Toronto on 29 April and went by the Great Western Railway to Detroit, and from there by the steamer *Illinois* to Grand Portage, at the mouth of the Pigeon River on Lake Superior. It was to get to Red River in 28 days from Grand Portage, or 34 days from Toronto. Indeed, so early did the party start and so rapidly did it press on, that it found Moose Lake a sheet of ice, which fortunately melted next day.

The difference in route was decided by the need to examine the passage by Pigeon River to Rainy River. This was the old North West Company route used before the drawing of the international boundary had put Grand Portage, then the depôt at Pigeon River, on American territory and forced a change to Fort William and the Kaministiquia River in 1804. The re-exploration of the Pigeon River route was the only part of Hind's expedition that overlapped Dawson's work. Hind was satisfied that he proved the route a more expeditious one by canoe, but the quickness of his party's travel may have owed something to the Iroquois and something more to the fact that Hind left Dawson's supplies at Fort William.

Arriving at Grand Portage on 5 May, the party took five days to carry their supplies up the long portage, but by 24 May they were again at Fort Frances and on 29 May at the mouth of the Winnipeg River. On 2 June Hind reached Dawson's headquarters in the Middle Settlement, and turned over the men and money to Dawson's deputy, the engineer and surveyor, Lindsay Russell. His having left the supplies at Lake Superior embarrassed Dawson, so much that his observations on the matter were the subject of a separate and unpublished communication to the Provincial Secretary in July. As Dawson had gone by Lake Manitoba to the lower Saskatchewan to ascertain the utility of that river for communication, the hostility of the two men, evident later, but perhaps earlier in origin and a reason for Hind's speed, was exacerbated, if not begun, by this episode.[6]

Hind was, however, in Red River and free to set out for the plains over three weeks earlier than the date of his departure from Toronto in 1857. He had certainly proved himself a master of organization and movement by canoe. From now on until he gave up field work about twenty years later, he was thoroughly at home in canoe and cart, on trail and in tent. He had entered the fellowship of the fur trader, the explorer, the field geologist.

It took some time, however, to prepare his party for the plains. For one thing, it had to be fairly large; the expedition up the Souris valley would take the explorers to the borders of the Sioux country, and fear of the Sioux was active in the settlement. But a few days before Hind reached Red River both buffalo hunters for the plains and trip-men for St. Paul had left the settlement, as they always did as soon as the grass had grown enough to feed their buffalo runners and oxen.

He thus had to seek out men and persuade them to join him. Provisions, moreover, were short, after the grasshoppers and the Canadian and British parties of 1857. For these reasons it took eight days to recruit eight men and the necessary provisions, carts, horses, and oxen.

By 14 June the caravan of five carts and one American wagon set out from the Middle Settlement for Fort Garry, to pick up flour and pemmican, the staple of travel in the Northwest. Its appearance was a bit odd even in that unconventional society: two light canoes had been put on the carts, as is done on motor cars today, to be used on the Saskatchewan. The caravan moved a half mile out on the prairies, in a modified 'Red River start,' and camped to make a last check of the arrangements.[7]

When the advance began next day, it had still to reach the real point of new departure. Hind, however, wished to add to his observation in 1857 of the Big Ridge. He therefore took part of the expedition, with Dickenson, northward along the ridge from St. James to Stony Mountain, a small limestone plateau rising slightly above the floor of the valley, and then westward to the Ridge itself. Part lake beach, part limestone plateau, it became one of the principal features of the Northwest as he saw it. The remainder of the party under Fleming followed the cart trail along the north bank of the Assiniboine to Portage.

There the two groups united, an old Cree hunter familiar with the prairies (unnamed) was added, and the party, now fifteen in number, struck out on 19 June into what was for Hind new country. The expedition of 1858 was at last actually in the field. Over it was to lie a quivering, yet constant haze of excitement, partly the result of alertness to the danger of the Sioux, but above all the inevitable response, stimulating or depressing, to the country itself. Hind now, for example, recorded the thrill of seeing from the Big Ridge, south across the treed course of the Assiniboine, what he had not noted in 1857, the thick hardwood and poplar forest lying dark between the Assiniboine itself and the Pembina escarpment far to the south. Exhilaration, an actual physical heightening of tension, also arose, as it still arises, from the clear atmosphere of the west with its crystalline luminosity and from the combination of the long sweep of the grasslands and the gentle elevations of the ridges and escarpments, both permitting and inviting a vast range of vision. The landscape, the skyscape, caught in their exquisite opalescence in Fleming's water colours,[8] had the vastness of ocean without ocean's monotony. And the open sweep of the landscape was varied and confirmed by the scattered isles of oaks and poplar, with occasionally continents of woods, such as that just mentioned, or the 'Bad Woods' west of Portage, an effect recorded in the names 'islets-de-bois' of the voyageurs and 'bluffs' of the half-breeds. This was the scene of the golden summer of Hind's life, a summer of command, of freedom, of achievement in work he was to do supremely well, noting and reporting the general features and possibilities of new country. In this year he also became one of the oddly recruited company of publicists, such as J.S. ('Saskatchewan') Taylor, who beckoned men on to new frontiers.

From Portage the party passed quickly over the prairie west of the settlement to the line of Rat Creek, and then followed the hunters' trail southwestward through the Bad Woods into the sandhills of the delta the Assiniboine had laid down in glacial Lake Agassiz, the precursor and parent of Lakes Winnipeg, Manitoba, and Winnipegosis. Its goal was the junction of the Assiniboine and the Souris, which it reached on 24 June. Hind, apparently not aware that the rainy season of the prairies was beginning, records, seemingly with some feeling of misfortune, the frequency and violence of the thunderstorms encountered. And he begins, in some of the memorable passages of the *Report* and the *Narrative*, to mention the strange, almost biblical, advance of the shimmering hordes of locusts out of the southwest.[9] The plague of 1857 had left even more numerous progeny. Hind was witnessing in the storms and locust swarms sweeping in from the southwest the sudden violence and teeming vitality of the prairies in right season and conjunction. In these and similar passages he brings to the account of his travels a strong tincture of the exotic glamour of the great African travel books of the time.

Passing up along the Souris southwestward through the great gorge at present-day Wawanesa, he began to search for the lignite and iron ores which, at his suggestion, he had been instructed to examine. Lignite boulders he found in plenty, but no beds in place; these were, he seems not to have realized, farther upstream at the present Estevan in Saskatchewan. Bog iron he found also, but not in significant amount. With these results, sufficient for a geologist, but not enough for a promoter, the party turned northward just above the boundary at the 49th parallel, and struck across the treeless prairie of the Souris to Fort Ellice on the Assiniboine. Burnt over the fall before, the prairie was verdant, but without wood - wood had to be carried and buffalo dung sought for the camp fires - and water was to be had only in the infrequent tributaries of the Souris. Buffalo herds also were absent. But so were the Sioux, despite an alarm while on the Souris and a probable attempt to steal the horses, thwarted by the keen watch of the Métis. Midway to the Assiniboine, a buffalo bull was found alone and shot, and, fortified by its strong-flavoured meat, the party came without incident or accident to Fort Ellice in the deep upland valley of the Assiniboine on 9 July. As Hind was to perceive later, he had crossed the southeastern corner of the short grass plains, the eastern angle of Palliser's famous triangle, which Hind himself adumbrated in his distinction between the country north and south of the Qu'Appelle River, the 'plains' and the 'prairies.'[10]

After three days refitting at Fort Ellice, the party, increased by one Indian guide, set out westward on the prairie south of the Qu'Appelle. For five days Hind noted the aridity and thundery summer weather of true prairie country, and the gathering of Indian turnips by squaws and children. He saw too, running at night, a prairie fire - 'put out,' as the phrase was, to turn the buffalo - and he noted its ravages, as he had those of the forest fires on Rainy River. Hind was not the only Canadian traveller to observe and reflect on the yearly fires and their denudation of the prairie and Shield country. He had now entered the country of the Plains Crees, horsed members of that far-flung tribe which had once proudly dominated the central prairies, and whom John W. McKay at Fort Ellice remembered coming to the post 'to receive their supplies, to the number of eight hundred warriors, splendidly mounted, and singing their war songs.'[11]

On its way the party met Charles Pratt, the country-born catechist of Qu'Appelle mission, and he offered it, with true half-breed hospitality, his young heifer at the mission to kill. On 17 July the travellers descended into the great valley of the Qu'Appelle at the Fishing Lakes where the mission was situated, conducted by the Rev. James Settee, an Anglican priest of the Swampy Cree tribe. Hind records his surprise at learning there that the vast trench ran straight westward undiminished until, except for a short intervening ridge, it almost joined with the South Saskatchewan River.[12] It is a matter for note that he had not learned this beforehand. As it was, the discovery was to give him one of his most persistent, and least feasible, ideas, that for an emigrant route by the South Saskatchewan to the Rockies.

His surprise seems the more remarkable in that he had planned to have the expedition break up at Qu'Appelle mission into three exploring parties, with a fourth group taking the carts and horses ahead to the Grand Forks of the Qu'Appelle where Long Lake drains in from the north. He had, that is, learned that he need no longer keep his party together in the country of the friendly Crees as he had had to do on the borders of that of the hostile Sioux. Dickenson with the guide obtained at Fort Ellice set out by canoe down the Qu'Appelle to explore its valley to the Assiniboine. Hime set out by land along the north bank of the Qu'Appelle valley to examine Long Lake and its land to the northwest. Hind and Fleming pushed by canoe through the other Fishing Lakes to follow the Qu'Appelle River westward towards the valley of the south branch of the Saskatchewan.[13] The vast area designated in Hind's instructions was to be encircled by canoe and quartered by cart, in what was clearly a well-planned use of men and time.

For four days Hind and Fleming pushed by canoe up the river swinging down its broad valley from 200 to 300 feet below the level of the plains above. These large and abrupt prairie valleys, cut by rivers long dry or dwindled, were one of the main features of the prairie west, and one of the chief worries of the later railway builders. Hind felt the sombre majesty of their rounded shoulders and their endless cleavage through the everlasting prairie land. Subsequently he was to see in the junction of the trough of the Qu'Appelle and the valley of the Saskatchewan an emigrants' route to the farther west, for he was already thinking of the new gold fields of British Columbia and of a third expedition as far at least as the Rockies in 1859.

To the reader of today, however, the chief interest of this section of the exploration is the encounter Hind had with the Plains Crees and what he wrote in his easy, vivid way of their life on the prairies. On 23 July his party camped for the night with six 'Bungays' - Indians of Cree and Ojibwa origin - who were making their way east. Next morning, however, they galloped after Hind and told him they wanted 'a little more talk.' Why, they wished to know, echoing the question put at Garden Island in 1857, was he travelling through their country? Hind on this occasion had the advantage of the services of his old plains hunter from Portage. When it became apparent that the Bungays were in fact demanding a toll for travelling on the plains, the old man told them that Hind's party had a large present for the chief of the Sandy Hills band, and would give no present except to him, as was the Indian custom. This knowledge of Indian protocol, and Hind's quiet unslinging of a gun, caused the Bungays quickly to turn back on their way. But they had said one true and important thing, that the Plains Crees, in council in 1857, had decided that, because of broken promises and the destruction of the buffalo, no white man or Métis should be allowed to hunt in their country or to travel in it except to trade in furs or pemmican and dried meat.[14] Hind was seeing clearly the signs of the imminent collapse of the old hunting economy of the Northwest and the unrest it was causing among the Indians. But although he faithfully recorded such experiences, and by reading as well as observation accumulated much on the Indians from Garden

Island to the Saskatchewan for his reports, he never spoke of a danger of Indian opposition to settlement as he did of Métis powers of resistance. Perhaps he saw none, yet fear of a rising of the Plains tribes was more than anything else a cause of anxiety in both the Red River and the Saskatchewan troubles later. Hind had perhaps too pleasant a time with the Sandy Hill Crees.

Certainly he was welcomed and feasted as he worked his way along the north height of the Qu'-Appelle valley, and was proudly taken to see the fly-blown horror of a pound filled with slaughtered and trampled buffalo. With Chief Shortstick, old as the plains themselves, he held prolonged council, he smoked many pipes in turn with the councillors, and he impressed, if not the impassive men, at least the chief's wives, with the 'good medicine' of the vesper match.[15] His is one of the best accounts of contacts with the Indians of the plains, not because his experience was extensive, but because he was respectful and sympathetic. Did he remember the folly of the evasiveness at Garden Island, and the grave Indian insistence on simple honesty? Or had he learned from the old hunter? At any rate his comments on Indian oratory, in style unchanged to this day, were, if amused, tolerant. 'They generally commenced with the creation, giving a short history of that event in the most general terms, and after a few flourishes about equality of origin, descended suddenly to buffaloes, half-breeds, the H.B. Company, tobacco and rum.'[16]

On 30 July the party examined the depression joining the Qu'Appelle and Saskatchewan valleys. Here Hind saw a possibility of diverting water from the Saskatchewan down the Qu'Appelle valley for either navigation or irrigation. It was a bold vision, to be dismissed by Dawson then and by John Macoun later as impracticable,[17] and realized even today only in part by the Saskatchewan (Gardiner) Dam. The group then descended to the broad river of the prairies and launched their now battered canoe on waters coming down from the Rockies. The South Saskatchewan slices through the prairies from its 'Elbow' to the junction with the North Saskatchewan like a giant knife and leaves exposed along its steep banks the strata of the sand and clay and boulders. It was a delight to Hind the geologist. In the party's identification of the widespread drift deposits and cretaceous formations of the plains, and its meeting to the northward of 'the woods,' the tree line at the edge of the parkbelt country in which the junction of North and South branches lies, were the two chief observations of the trip. The chief incident was a sleepless night spent watching for a grizzly bear; that great brute of uncertain temper was still a danger of the prairies.

The 'swift-flowing' river soon carried the light canoe down to the meeting of the branches. Hind and Fleming strove against the strong current of the North Saskatchewan to test its quality, and then turned down the main river to the Church of England mission of Nipawin opposite the site of the old French Fort à la Corne. On 7 August they were welcomed there by the Rev. Henry Budd, first native priest of the Church of England in Rupert's Land, and Hind recognized the need for his mission labours, and also the fertility of the land round about.

Hind had now skirted in his track of exploration from the Souris at the boundary line to the South Saskatchewan, the borderland between what he later defined in his *Narrative* as 'prairie' and as 'plain.' The latter was the short grass country of 'Palliser's triangle,' and Hind was to realize it was not generally suitable for settlement, as settlement and agriculture then were. It was a broad perception, but it was not a scientific insight. He had not yet, however, recognized the significance, as a 'fertile belt,' of the 'prairie' or parkbelt country. At Nipawin he was well within it, and had left the 'provisions' or 'buffalo plains' behind him, to enter the wooded country of the fur trade.

  Yet Hind had a strong strategic sense of exploration, as his dispositions now made clear. He boldly, almost rashly, sent Fleming with two voyageurs to follow the old fur route of the Saskatchewan to Lake Winnipeg, and the lake itself to Red River. He would thus obtain a report on the northern and eastern limit of the region his party was to explore. He himself, with carts and ponies procured at Nipawin, began on 9 August the long trek from the Saskatchewan south to Fort Ellice on the Assiniboine, and on by what was soon to be called the North Trail by the southern flank of Riding Mountain and the White Mud River to Portage and Red River. Hime and Dickenson he picked up at Fort Ellice, the latter having explored northward as far as Fort Pelly in the upper Assiniboine valley. On this trek Hind saw a long stretch of parkbelt country and grasped its suitability for settlement. But his acute powers of observation and description failed to rise to the magnificent perceptions of the grand design of the patterns of plain and parkbelt. Hind had seen the prairies intimately and with all their bold elements, but he had not fully grasped the broad and simple pattern those elements made up. Perhaps he needed, as Palliser was doing, to travel as far as the Rockies to see the pattern completed.

  His party, now experienced trip-men, passed quickly from Fort Ellice to Red River through what he correctly predicted would some day be settled country - great-grandparents of the writer settled along Hind's route only thirteen years later - and by 4 September was once more in Red

River. An expedition of nearly three months had been conducted without mishap or hardship, with all its objects accomplished. It was a good performance, even if it rested on the skill and endurance of voyageur and plainsman, and on the lightness and reparability of the all-wood Red River cart and the forest-made birch bark canoe.

Such good fortune failed young John Fleming on his voyage by the Saskatchewan and Lake Winnipeg; he suffered many hardships and dangers, including near starvation, before he reached Red River on 16 September.[18]

Nevertheless, within two days Fleming set out again with Hind to return a third of the distance up Lake Winnipeg on a journey to examine the salt springs of Lake Winnipegosis, one of the special objects of the expedition, and to look over the country on the way. Hind had spent the two weeks since his return in writing reports and preparing for the journey to Winnipegosis, while Hime made his strong black and white photographs of Red River scenes.[19] He also had had Dickenson prepare to explore the country between the Lake of the Woods, the Red and the Assiniboine rivers, and the boundary.

On 18 September Hind's party began the last phase of the explorations by York boat. It must be assumed that Hime was with the group if only to explain the photograph of Susan, the maidenly Swampy half-breed, which appears in colour in the *Narrative*. They made their way down the Red and through the fickle weather of Lake Winnipeg to the mouth of the Little Saskatchewan (now Fairford) River, by which they passed to Lake Manitoba. Here Hind traversed the flat limestone reaches that embed the great lakes of the Winnipeg basin, and create a waste country of shallow waters, spreading marshes, and thin soils. Here also at Fairford Mission on St. Martin's Lake he met Miss Harriet

Thompson of Nottingham, who gave him a few numbers of the *Nottingham Journal*, and must have talked of the Stoney Gate and the market with him.[20] He reflected on the action of ice in pushing boulders ashore, which he was to observe again on Lakes Winnipegosis and Dauphin – the beginning of one of his main lines of thought. From St. Martin's Lake the travellers followed the Little Saskatchewan to Lake Manitoba, that body of water which so soon was to give its name to a new province of a new Canada. They took then the bent-pin course of the Waterhen River into Lake Winnipegosis. There on its west shore they examined the salt springs where the Monkman family had been making salt for some years. The brine flowed from the porous limestone beds, of course, and salt was easily, if crudely, evaporated. Like the lignite of the Souris, it might be useful for settlers, but the abundance of salt did not tell much more than was already known of the geological composition of the country.

Hind was more interested, and rightly, in the blue fronts of the escarpment rising abruptly to the west, the Riding, Duck, and Porcupine mountains standing in three bluff bastions from south to north. The escarpment was a bold exercise in earth moulding, and tempted Hind, as it still tempts the tourist, to climb its heights and turn to see the vast stretch of lake and level from which it rises. Hind and Fleming continued to ascend to the Mossy River to Lake Dauphin and from its southwestern sandy beach made their way by marsh and fertile prairie to the great gravel ridge Hind had already noted on his journey from Fort Ellice to Red River. Then by more marsh and prairie they came to the foot of Riding Mountain and scrambled up its steep and wooded eastern slope. At the top they were in the heavy ('thick-wood') forest that blanketed the plateau. From its shoulder they gazed eastward and north in a Pisgah view of prairie, marsh, and lake laid out in a vast mosaic below and growing dim in ever deepening blue towards the greater lakes, the enormous fragments of the glacial sea that had once lapped the escarpment and had left the ridge running clear below, like a cast-off cloak dropped in its millennial ebb. The look-out gave Hind his best perception of the structure and texture of the immense tract of country he had traversed, and he gained there the insight that was to give his report its chief value, a comprehension of the formation of the lands he was to recommend to be settled or to be avoided. 'The result obtained by the ascent of the Riding Mountain,' he wrote, 'has been of great interest in a geological point of view, since it has unlocked in a great measure the geology of this region of country.'[21]

The date was 10 October, and when the party awoke on the high plateau the next morning, snow lay six inches deep on the ground. It was time to set out on the long way back to Red River and to Canada, even if the Indian summer of the prairie was to cast its enchantment over the rest of their stay in the Northwest and lull the onset of winter. Fleming, ever the faithful Achates of the expedition, took the boat back to Lake Manitoba. Hind struck east on foot across the lowlands to Manitoba House on the lake of that name, and observed the features of this strange, drowned country so recently emerged from the ghostly waters of Agassiz. On 25 October he camped on an island to intercept Fleming, and during his three nights there heard the bell-like tinkle of the waves in the limestone overhang of the lake's shores, which gave it its name, 'the speaking spirit.' From the island they coasted by the east shore to Oak Point, and there took the trail to Red River, which Hind reached on 30 October.

The season was so late that Hind had to prepare to return to railhead, in what had just that year become the state of Minnesota, by winter travel by snowshoe and dogsled. The necessity was at least to add a lively chapter to his *Narrative* and another description of life and travel in the Northwest. It is true that if he had set out immediately he could still have reached Crow Wing by cart, but he had to collect Dickenson, whose explorations south of the Assiniboine are not mentioned in the *Report* or *Narrative*, assemble and pack the specimens of rock fossils, plants, etc., the expedition had collected, and engage a party of winter tripmen. The whole month of November was spent in preparation - Hind did find time to lecture in Red River[22] - and it was not until 30 November that the whips cracked to start the dogs trotting on the white trail to Pembina and Crow Wing.

Much interest was added to the month of preparation and to the novel journey by the belated arrival in Red River at the end of October of a party of young English noblemen to hunt buffalo, among them Lord Frederick Cavendish (later to be assassinated in Phoenix Park, Dublin) with whom thereafter Hind claimed acquaintance. They succeeded in getting their buffaloes near Devil's Lake in what is now North Dakota, and Lord Richard Grosvenor also made a journey to Fort Ellice and the Plains Crees of the Qu'Appelle.[23] The entire party then prepared to go east in the same way and along the same route as Hind. Inevitably a race developed among the members of the united parties, pressed so hard one marvels that Hind could make the observations for the vivid and lively chapter that closes his *Narrative*. (His observations may explain his coming in third.) By 28 December 1858 Hind was back in Toronto.[24] The great expedition had closed with a dash.

Hind then resumed his teaching, much neglected, at Trinity College, and his activities in the Royal Canadian Institute. He had ceased to be a member of the editorial committee, but was made Librarian in 1859. In April of that year he published a paper in the *Canadian Journal*, 'Of Some of the Superstitions and Customs Common among the Indians in the Valley of the Assiniboine and Saskatchewan.' He read a paper at the December meeting of the institute on 'The Distribution of Clay Iron-stone in the Cretaceous Rocks of Rupert's Land in the North-West Territory.' In his address to the institute in 1859, President G.W. Allan found, with much to praise, Hind's report of 1858 on the summer weather of Red River 'a matter of surprise' - as it was, the figures being incorrect.[25] In short, Hind was living again in his familiar Toronto setting.

He was busy also at the preparation of his second report, one which was to outdo the first in size and comprehensiveness. Again he marshalled instructions, reports of progress, a record of the explorations based on his field notebooks, the reports of Dickenson and Fleming, and then added separate chapters on the inhabitants, geology, climatology, and agricultural possibilities, with maps, sections of rivers, tables of rainfall, all supported with copious extracts from and references to leading authorities. The report was a masterpiece of compilation, and all of it was readable. Like the report of 1857, it placed the expedition of 1858 securely in the bibliography of Canadian historiography and North American geography. But, also like the report of 1857, it at once owed too much to others, yet placed Hind firmly in the forefront of the Canadian explorers. A sympathetic newspaper could refer to him as though he had been the Palliser of the Canadian exploration of the Northwest.[26]

Hind's exuberance in using others' work, his tendency to place himself in the spotlight as explorer and writer, were to have their consequences. As the report of 1858 was to prove the peak of Hind's achievement during his career, one may ask what in fact he had accomplished by the two expeditions and reports? He had been organizer, explorer, observer, botanist, meteorologist, geologist, writer. If the first three may be grouped under the one term 'explorer,' Hind had done well. He had learned to travel fast, to have what was needed, to be cool in danger, to see and analyse, to note accurately and report in context. He is to be ranked with the great African travellers, even if the Northwest was an easier and more peaceful region than central Africa. As a botanist, he was no more than competent, if that, and somewhat failed to grasp the significance of the extent and variation of 'prairie' and 'plain,' attributing to fire what was mainly the effect of light and varying rainfall. Similarly, as a meteorologist he failed to read correctly the results of his and other weather records and observations of rainfall. In consequence he exaggerated both the rainfall and the warmth of the Northwest in his reports, although he carefully corrected the errors in the British editions of them.[27] His failure to see, like Macoun later, that what really mattered was the amount of rainfall, highly variable, and the actual length of the period free of frost in any given season, is another, perhaps the principal, example of his failure to squeeze the most from the masses of material he had assembled.

It was, however, geology that claimed his allegiance as a scientist, and it is really by his chapter on the geology of the region he explored that he is to be judged. First to be noted is his quite unusual capacity to depict on a broad scale the geological features of the country he traversed.

From the Precambrian rock stretching from Fort William to the mouth of the Winnipeg River, the limestone of the Winnipeg basin and the Red River valley, to the cretaceous formations of what is now called the Manitoba escarpment, he builds up the fundamental structure of the regions as it is known today. Here he proved himself to be more than an amateur, rather a well-trained, if self-educated, professional. In his powers of analysis he is not, however, to be ranked with other self-trained men, such as James Richardson of Lower Canada or G.F. Matthew of New Brunswick. He was always more concerned to describe graphically than to analyse scientifically.

When one turns, moreover, to either specific discovery or to general insight, one is disappointed. On the former, Sir William Logan is a sure reference. Although no longer trustful of Hind when his great *Geology of Canada* was published in 1863, it is evident that he sought painstakingly to record both fairly and precisely what Hind had done as a geologist in his explorations to the northwest. The sum is startlingly small: '... by his explorations in the Red River region he [Hind] had shown the extension in that direction of the Lower Silurian and Devonian series, without the intervention of the Middle and Upper Silurian,' the absence of the two formations being the point. Hind had also sent back fossils to F.B. Meek and Elkanah Billings of the Geological Survey for identification; these were gratefully acknowledged, and two were named after him, *Cyrtodonta hindi* and *Leda hindi*.[28]

Warren Upham, in his study of 1895, *The Glacial Lake Agassiz*, was more appreciative, making no less than fourteen references to Hind's work, and especially agreeing with Hind's theory that the beds of the lakes of the Winnipeg basin had been excavated from the limestone. But even Upham's citations point up Hind's failure - although the term is perhaps too harsh - to see then what is now so clear. Noting glacial action on both the Shield and the prairies and aware of Agassiz's theory of continental glaciation, he nevertheless fell short of formulating a theory of glacial action in the region he explored, though it is true many leading geologists were still reluctant to adopt the theory of continental glaciation.[29] Aware that the Red River valley had once been a great lake, he failed to address himself to the problem of trying to explain its origin. Aware also of the distinction between the arid southwestern plains and the northeastern and northern parkbelt, he did not give a broad, graphic description of the difference, as Palliser's report almost casually did in its phrase of 3 August 1858, 'the fertile belt.'[30] Hind, it would seem, was a sharp observer and faithful describer, but he lacked the imaginative power - perhaps as a result of his want of formal training - to see fundamental relationships. He possessed, in short, a second rate, if speculative mind.

While Hind was preparing his second report, he was also busying himself in attempting to organize a third expedition, this time one by the Bow River to the Rockies. His interest now had shifted, from settlement to migration to British Columbia, a shift to be explained by the news from the goldfields there, and the possibility of gold being found on the eastern slopes of the Rockies. Hind believed he had traced as far as the Elbow of the South Saskatchewan a possible emigrant trail, which could be continued by that river and the Bow to the passes of the mountains.[31] A third expedition would complete the Canadian parallel with the Palliser expedition, and was not unreasonable. But the depression of 1857 had left the Canadian government wary of making further expenditures on explorations that duplicated the British ones. And Sir William Logan was not ready to send Richardson as geologist, if a third expedition was planned.[32] Why Hind should have been out of the running is not clear, but it is possible that the suspicion with which Logan regarded him later had had its beginning with the too ambitious report of 1857. It is possible also that the report of 1858 was causing doubt in government and scientific circles. At any rate, from the beginning of 1859 one can sense that while Hind's reputation stood at its peak, opposition to his further employment had begun to form.

Certainly if the suspicion arose from the feeling that he was disposed to make too much of his own, and other men's, work, the history of the publication of the 1858 report sustains the view that he was so inclined. Simon Dawson, no longer a friend of Hind but a critic, said that the appearance of the report was delayed because Hind had exceeded the limits as to size and maps that had been imposed, no doubt for economy's sake. (The report of Simon Dawson's own expedition of 1858, on the other hand, was published in 1859.) A new order from the Speaker had to be obtained before the report as Hind had prepared it could be published. The result was that it did not appear until early in 1860, although finished and tabled before the Legislature earlier, and dated in its published form 1859.[33] Once again Hind had pushed his work beyond agreed limits.

To explain a situation which was in effect a conflict with Dawson, it is necessary, however, to note that the Canadian explorations of the Northwest had been a great effort at expansion, and there were people eager to exploit the new possibilities. The explorations themselves had been forced on a government, at least doubtful it not reluctant, by the pressure of the Toronto expansionists led by Allan McDonell. They were in touch with Lord Bury, son-in-law of Sir Allan

Macnab, and with Hugh Allan of Montreal. They had
wanted a Canadian route to Red River, a Canadian
settlement there, and, by 1858, fired by the gold
rush in British Columbia, a route to the Pacific.
In August 1858 they formed the North-West Transportation Company (reorganized in 1860 as the
North-West Transit Company). William MacDonell
Dawson was its first president. The company pur-
chased the steamer *Rescue* to ply from Collingwood
to Fort William, and in 1859 obtained a subsidy
from the Canadian government to carry mail to
Red River. This it did for one year. The service
was unreliable and the subsidy was withdrawn in
1860.[34] The attempt promised, however, to make a
Canadian route to Red River possible, and so gain
for the entrepreneurs a commanding position in
opening a route to British Columbia.

In 1859, therefore, the expansionists were at
full strain after the prize they had started to
pursue in 1857. There is no reason to think that
in 1857 Hind had any difference with them; indeed
Sandford Fleming, Hind's friend, had been one of
the undertakers of the North-West Transportation
Company. Rivalry between Hind and the Dawsons, however, had developed, or was thought by the latter
to have developed.[35] The available evidence, fragile though it is, at least indicates how the
Dawsons could have become suspicious of Hind. Hind
had in March 1858, as noted, visited Sir George
Simpson at Lachine, to request assistance in obtaining Iroquois canoemen and letters of introduction to Hudson's Bay Company men in the Northwest.
To make such a visit was only sensible. The Hudson's
Bay Company and its governors, however, were thought
by the Toronto expansionists and the *Globe* to be
actively opposed to the acquisition by Canada of
Rupert's Land, and to be influencing the Liberal-
Conservative government to delay any action to
bring about the transfer of the Northwest to Canada.

Indeed, the *Globe* regarded the expeditions themselves as deliberate and unnecessary delays, especially that of 1858.[36]

In the course of 1859 the Dawsons became convinced that Hind was both shaping his report to serve the interests of the Hudson's Bay Company rather than their own, and opposing them even to the point, so it was alleged, of urging the use of the American route by St. Paul, instead of that within Canadian territory,[37] none of which Hind's second report does. Nothing more is available to fill out this account of their hostility, although it would seem Hind favoured at this time a route by the South Saskatchewan, Dawson one by the North. It is important, however, in that the hostility may have affected the decision not to use Hind on the contemplated expedition of 1859. Thus Hind was not to be employed, while Dawson continued his survey of the Superior-Red River route. Clearly Hind had gained rivals as well as fame in the Northwest.

The suspicion, to say no more, that Hind was unscrupulous in the use of other men's findings and material remained, and was to harden. That suspicion was to be confirmed by the publication of his *Narrative* in 1860. The extent of his hasty appropriation of the work of others remains to be assessed. What cannot be doubted is that he displayed the publicist's ability to take data collected and organized by others and put them in striking phrases. The outstanding example at this time was his seizing on the term 'fertile belt' and printing it with capitals and without acknowledgment in the preface to his *Narrative*.[38] He had plagiarized the key phrase that would unlock the Northwest. In doing so, Hind revealed what was emerging as his authentic self, that of what today would be called a publicist and a promoter. He used his scientific skills and his explorations to point to new resources and invite men to develop them. He was not, in fact, the restrained professional scientist like Logan, Hunt, Croft, or Chapman. He was first and foremost the frontier publicist, the promoter of new ventures. As such, he would be distrusted by the scientists. As such, he still had a certain role to play in his time.

 Hind had, in short, tasted the delights of exploration and of publication, and was never to lose his love of the campfire and the page proof. He had found his occupation, and a formula: quickly to explore, report, and publish. The rest of his active life was to be an attempt to repeat the achievement of 1857-1860. It was to be ironic that, because of the reputation he had gained among his fellow scientists, the Northwest was to be closed to him henceforward.

v The Search for Fame
1860 – 1864

The great expeditions and his reports set Hind on a quest for a more distinguished, and perhaps a more profitable career than he had yet achieved. He remained, it is true, a professor of Trinity College during these years; he continued to be active in the Royal Canadian Institute and to publish in the *Canadian Journal*. His happy home life went its quiet course; his family grew. Hind had, however, found the way of life which satisfied at once his curiosity and his ambition: to explore, to report, to publish. Like many more famous Victorians, he wanted to see the unknown parts of the world so rapidly opening to the steamship and the hunting rifle, and to write in bold, Ruskinian prose of their colour and their marvels.

The years from 1860 to 1864 are, therefore, marked by repeated efforts to explore and to publish, to publish not only learned papers, but books that would sell, as his *Narrative* was to do.[1] At first he continued to seek support for a trip to explore an emigrants' route by the South Saskatchewan and Bow rivers to the southern passes of the British American Rockies, the passes then being explored by Palliser. In October 1859 he wrote to the Colonial Secretary, the Duke of Newcastle, both to return the proofs of his 1858 report, which was being published by the imperial government, and to request the support of the Colonial Office for the Bow River expedition, at a cost of £2000 sterling.[2] The duke replied that, in view of the expenditures made on Palliser's expeditions, no further outlay was contemplated. The Canadian government, moreoever, refused to support his application,[3] and this reply closed the door on further western exploration by Hind.

As he had no journey to the Rockies to prepare for, he might well have been content to emphasize his neglected teaching in 1860. His other activities, however, continued. In April he read before the Royal Canadian Institute a paper 'On the Occurrence of Grasshoppers (so called) in the Northwest.' He again became librarian of the institute. The favourable notice of his reports in the *Canadian Journal*, a summary with copious extracts, must have given him satisfaction after the brush with the Dawsons.[4] Equally satisfying must have been the news of his election as a Fellow of the Royal Geographical Society in 1859.[5] And during the time since the completion of his report of 1858, he had been adapting and adding to both his reports for publication as a narrative. When the book manuscript was completed and accepted by Longmans is unknown, but negotiations must have been concluded during the winter of 1859-60. It was desirable for Hind to go to England to see his great work through the press.

So, for the first time since he had left in 1846, Hind returned to England. He went in midsummer to correct his formal reports for their second publication, and to confer with John Arrowsmith, the famous map-maker. One may assume that he also visited his mother and brothers in Nottingham, perhaps suppose that he attended meetings of the Royal Geographical Society, which in its *Journal*

of 1860 published a summary of his 1858 *Report*.
The important thing, however, must have been that
he was encouraged by his success as a writer to
attempt on his return another application of his
formula of exploration and publication.

When his *Narrative of the Canadian Red River
Exploring Expedition of 1857 and of the Assiniboine
and Saskatchewan Exploring Expedition of 1858* appeared in two volumes, one year after Charles
Darwin's *The Origin of Species*, three years before
H.J. Speke's *Journal of the Discovery of the Source
of the Nile*, it easily fell into step with the wide
procession of Victorian publications on science and
discovery. The *Narrative* was a good example of a
kind of book popular in its day and readily entered
the fellowship of nineteenth century travel books.
It was favourably, if not widely, reviewed in, for
example, the *Edinburgh Review* and the *Morning
Chronicle*. The latter wrote, 'This is a noble work'
and praised it highly. In Canada, Daniel Wilson
gave it in the *Canadian Journal* a copious and entirely favourable review.[6]

The *Chronicle*'s praise was somewhat exaggerated.
The *Narrative* is the two earlier reports, less formal, more colourful, with fewer details, tables,
references, and dates, and more broad description,
but substantially the reports. It indeed seems indisputable that Hind wrote the reports with the
Narrative in mind. For example, the report for
1857 (p. 245) has a description of different aspects of the falls of the Winnipeg River 'in the
grey dawn of morning, or rose-coloured by the
setting sun, or flashing in the brightness of noon
day, or silvered by the soft light of the moon.'
So does the *Narrative* (I, 107). The reports were
written to be the *Narrative*; the *Narrative* is the
reports, pruned for popular reading. This fact is
convincing evidence that Hind was working from
1857 to 1860 to the Victorian formula of explore

and publish, as he was to do thereafter.

For this formula, the *Narrative* was a success, if by no means a triumph. It is unknown how many copies were sold; the British Museum records a second edition, but this writer has seen no copy of it. In any case, Hind was encouraged to go on to explore and publish further. He was justified in the attempt. The *Narrative* is first rate of its kind as a perceptive description of lands which, if known for over half a century, were to most people only vaguely known. Particularly was this true of the Canadian prairies. The fur traders had kept to the northern forests, and the explorers such as Franklin and Richardson had followed the routes of the fur trade. Hind had first presented, with the vividness which was his peculiar gift, the wide spaces and deep valleys of the grass and aspen country of the west. The *Narrative* was like a ship bursting into unknown seas. As such it remains at once a source of much and various detail and a brilliant description of the plains on the eve of settlement.

During a further year at Trinity, Hind was still librarian of the Institute, and became editor of the *Journal of the Board of Arts and Manufactures for Upper Canada*, a routine job in which he did little writing.[7] In January 1861 he read before the institute his 'Remarks on Indian Art,' illustrated by a collection of Indian relics obtained during the Assiniboine and Saskatchewan expedition, and in February a paper 'On the Manufacture of Shale Oil from the Utica Slate of Collingwood.'[8] Among these occupations and with such encouragement, he planned a new expedition. The northwest being now closed, he turned to the northeast.

No other reason is known for his choice of Labrador for an expedition, except that his attention was drawn to the Moisie, or Grand, River by Abbé J.B.A. Ferland,[9] perhaps as a way to the

Hamilton Inlet and the sea. It may have been merely that all the country north of the St. Lawrence lowlands was even more unknown to Canadians of that day than the Northwest. What is known is that Hind tried to have the provincial government, now sitting once more in Quebec City, make his project an official expedition. It refused to do so, perhaps because there was no pressure such as had launched the expedition to the northwest, but no doubt also because its finances were still strained. It did, however, appoint two surveyors, veterans of the journeys to the Northwest, Edward Cayley and J.F. Gaudet, to accompany the expedition. But there is no minute of the Executive Council approving payment; Hind seems to have met the costs of the party from his own resources. Perhaps that is why Hind's brother, W.G.R. Hind, accompanied the expedition as sketcher and artist, even if Paul Kane had been interested in the same work.[10] The party assembled at Quebec City and on 4 June 1861 left for the mouth of the Moisie River, 400 miles down the St. Lawrence. There they would buy canoes and engage canoemen for the trip inland.

The only known surviving account of the expedition is Hind's book, *Explorations in the Interior of the Labrador Peninsula*. As it was not, except for the two surveyors from the Crown Lands Department, a government expedition, there was no need for a formal report like those of 1857 and 1858. Hind had no instructions, and the purpose of his expedition is not explicitly stated by him. It may, however, be discerned from the book. His plan was to ascend the Moisie, which comes down from the Labrador tableland in a generally straight course from north to south. On this ascent it would be possible to take a cross section of the peninsula and to learn something from the Indians, to whome the Moisie was an ancient route, of the interlocking of its headwaters with those of the

Grand River which flowed into Hamilton Inlet on the Atlantic coast. The project thus offered a good field reconnaissance for the brief Labrador summer; it would allow a maximum of observation for a minimum of exacting Labrador travel. In fact, however, the 'interior' was only just reached, and there is some possibility Hind turned back before he had achieved all that he had hoped.

The Indians of the St. Lawrence coast were reluctant to engage for what they knew would be a toilsome trip, but on 10 June 1861 the party, consisting of the four 'gentlemen' noted above, six French Canadian voyageurs, and an Abenaki and a Montagnais, set out in three canoes up the at first broad and level but soon to be rapid-torn Moisie. Once more the adventurous Hind was in the field, filling his leather-bound notebooks from which a new set of twin volumes would emerge.

The character of the river soon changed as the canoes reached the foot of its descent down the steep southern front of the Labrador tableland, which rose some 2,000 feet from sea leavel in no more than 150 miles. The Great Rapids of the Moisie were the first and principal impediment, but from there on the canoes were tracked and portaged almost as much as paddled, through the turbulent current and five other rapids of the river. To follow the route of the Montagnais hunters was no small feat of canoe and wood craft, and to take the levels of the boldly rising country was a constant task for the surveyors. Hind's narrative is vivid with accounts of the difficulties and dangers of a canoe trip far more trying than the passage of the Winnipeg River.

By 30 June the party had reached the headwaters of the Moisie. On 1 July it crossed the edge of the tableland with its shallow streams, dangerous to the fragile canoes. There the rapidly falling summer water, and the impossibility of going by foot across the moss-covered rocks and muskeg of the tableland to the tributaries of the Grand River, except at a heavy cost in toil to the men and in the face of a lack of game and fish, made Hind determined to return to the coast by the Moisie. The decision probably meant, although this is not said in the book, a defeat of the ultimate hopes of the enterprise. Like a good explorer, having made the decision to return, Hind carried it out quickly. On 2 July the descent began. Quicker, but little less difficult and dangerous than the ascent, the downward journey ended at Moisie Bay on 8 July.

The 'exploration' was, in the result, no more than a difficult reconnaissance inland. Hind had obviously hoped to go farther, perhaps to descend the Grand River to Hamilton Inlet. But he had barely reached the interior, much less explored it. It is perhaps this falling short of expectations that was to give his book an effect of being somewhat padded and stretched out: a one and a half volume book has been expended to the necessary two. Hind himself considered it to be written in 'a more popular style.'[11]

Nevertheless, the first volume of the *Explorations in Labrador* is not inferior in interest and readability to the *Narrative* of the northwestern expeditions. The description of the country is as effectively done, perhaps more so, mountains and valleys being always more picturesque than plains. The rocky character of Labrador, essentially a vast slab of Precambrian stone, the bold, rounded shoulders of the mountain ridges, the heavy scatter of boulders, the tumbled, shallow-rooted forests, the quick water of early summer, the ever present moss, the mosquitoes and the blackflies: all these Hind keeps constantly before his readers. He spends much more time than in the *Narrative* on the members of his party, particularly on the Montagnais, Louis, he of the ever hopeless life and the unhappy marriage,

and on the Indians of the peninsula. From Louis
and from Indians met en route, notably Kewayden,
he learned much of the way of life, the history,
and the wanderings of the Montagnais and the Naskapis, the two tribes of the interior of Labrador.
Valuable as Hind's accounts of the Plains Crees
were, it is possible that in these records of the
Labrador Indians he did a better service than in
his former work.

The book is marked also by a recurrence of a
theme in the *Narrative*, the effects of fire. In
an imaginative and perceptive account of its relation
to the forests and soil of Labrador,[12] Hind portrayed
what was true both on the Canadian prairie and in
the Canadian forest: that fire was an active and
constant agent in both environments and one of the
determinants of their character. The intense summer heat, the quick growth and quick curing of
prairie grass and Labrador moss created ready conditions for wild fire in grassland and woodland.
To this readiness was added the habit of the
Plains Indians of deliberately 'putting out' fire,
and the lumberman's burning of slash. Thus with
the harsh climate of the plains and the plateau
was combined, rather paradoxically, the fierce dash
of the running flames. Hind's realization that fire
was a constant historical factor in Canada is revealed by his quick research of accounts of the
'Dark Days' of Canada, days when the settlements
in the St. Lawrence valley were darkened by smoke
from the burning woods and muskegs in the wilderness to the north. The whole chapter is perhaps
the best example of Hind's ability to combine his
own observations and descriptive powers with research to make his account of a topic vivid and
memorable.

This first volume amounts, then, to a graphic
description of the Moisie valley and the people
who travelled through it, a description done not

only in Hind's prose, but in his brother's paintings, notably, 'The Third Rapid on the Moisie,' the frontispiece. The summer majesty, the winter solitude of the vast plateau, its tortuous river systems, the silent boulders and grey acres of caribou moss, the archaic continuance of the world before life, were somehow caught in this tableau of a toilsome June.

Back at Moisie Bay, Hind and his party, less the surveyors, turned to an examination of the north shore of the Gulf of St. Lawrence and its developing fisheries. These were almost as old as New France, but the Reciprocity Treaty of 1854, settlement along the north shore, the coming of the steamship, and the Grand Trunk Railway running on the south shore to Rivière du Loup, had kindled new hopes of their greater development. By 22 July Hind had made his way along the coast as far east as Mingan; he returned to Quebec by ship in August.[13] From this two-week examination he produced a useful account of the Indians, settlers, missions, and fisheries of the north shore, their past and present, supporting it by a mass of fishing statistics. His is a valuable, often graphic description of a little known part, even today, of Canada. It rounded out the second volume, and introduced Hind to yet another interest of his later life, the Atlantic fisheries. The geologist of the plains was in due course to become also a student of 'ocean physics.'

At the annual meeting of the Royal Canadian Institute in December 1861, Hind, re-elected librarian, read a paper, 'A Communication Embodying Observations made during his Expedition to the Labrador Coast in the Summer of 1861.'[14] It was one sign of another busy year of teaching, meeting his small classes at Trinity, and publishing. His *A Sketch of an Overland Route to British Columbia*, with a letter from Sandford Fleming as an appendix, appeared in 1862. The pamphlet, written to help the Overlanders of 1862, was a return to his interest in the Northwest, and an indication that it had by no means died on the coast of Labrador. It had a special personal interest too: his brother William had joined the Canadian party of Overlanders to go to British Columbia and add to his sketches and paintings of British America. Henry Youle was still firmly a frontier expensionist and was becoming a Canadian nationalist, in short a promoter, as his future activities were again to show. Indeed, the second volume of his *Labrador* pointed clearly to the same concerns. And most of the winter and summer of 1862 must actually have been devoted to the writing of the *Labrador*. There is no indication that he went to England to see it through the press. It was received without extensive comment.

The year 1862 was not a prosperous one for Canada, or for Hind. The depression ran on; the business boom caused by the American Civil War had not yet reached the British American provinces. Financial stringency came all too readily into the sheltered cloisters of Trinity College. Its historian notes that by the end of 1862 retrenchment was necessary: 'the college laundry was discontinued, resident students were required to pay for the coal consumed in their fireplaces, and beer was an extra charge in the college accounts.' Clearly matters were grave, but worse accompanied these blows. The salaries of the Provost and Professor Hind were cut by £100 each for 1862-1863.[15] Such are the needs of small colleges! It was no doubt calculated that the Provost and Hind could best afford the reductions. Hind perhaps because of his summer earnings in 1857 and 1858 and the royalties from his *Narrative*. As it may have been, however, that the inadequacy of his salary made him, in part at least, a writer for gain, the cut was some-

what unkind. It is possible there may have been
some dissatisfaction about the time Hind gave to
his extra-mural interests, even some jealousy of
it. However that may be, 1863 saw an unprecedented
burst of activity on Hind's part, and the session
of 1863-1864 was to be his last at Trinity.

For the session 1862-63 Hind soldiered on, still
showing the curious variety of his inquiries. In late
1863 he was to read a paper before the institute,
'On Vegetable Parchment, its Uses and Preparation.'[16]
Otherwise, the session was uneventful, but during
its passage he must have planned, if not worked
on, another major work that was to appear in 1863:
his *Eighty Years' Progress of British North America*,
edited and in part written by himself, with special
articles by others. It was a useful and promotional
survey of material progress in Canada since the
American Revolution. In no sense was it a book by
Hind, but a large-scale compilation of the kind at
which he had become skilful. It made its mark,
however, and called for a new edition, with a pre-
fatory sketch and retitled *The Dominion of Canada*,
in 1869. The preface of *Eighty Years' Progress*
displays Hind as an eloquent nationalist, a jour-
nalistic father of Confederation. He urged British
North Americans to lay 'broad and deep the founda-
tions of a new nationality ... a nationality whose
future should witness the consolidation and growth,
on this continent, of those principles of British
colonial freedom, which are so eminently calculated
to promote internal peace and prosperity, and under God's blessing, the enjoyment also of "life
and liberty," as well as the "pursuit of happiness"
among all classes of people.'[17]

This was a sudden flowering indeed of the expansionist spirit expressed in Hind's explorations,
and no specific reason is known why he should
suddenly have become an advocate of Confederation.
But beyond doubt 1863 was Hind's year as prophet

of Canadian nationality. In May appeared the first number of the *British American Magazine*, with Hind as editor. Who inspired its foundation, or paid its initial expenses, is unknown. It is unlikely that Hind did the latter, although he may have done the former. The new periodical was a typical Victorian 'magazine,' a collection of essays, stories, poems, and reviews. Despite the fact that its first number appeared without editorial or manifesto, it was clearly meant to be nationalist in tone and context. Its first article was by the editor, on 'North-West British America.' In the opening paragraphs Hind wrote of the danger of the absorption of the Northwest by 'a Northern federation and the annihilation of hopes long cherished by British American people that *their empire* will one day be established from ocean to ocean, in peaceful union with the empire from which they have sprung.' He quoted annexationist statements from the Americans, James Wickes Taylor and Salmon P. Chase.[18] The rest of the article, which was continued in the next number, is merely descriptive, but the nationalist tone, so clearly sounded, was kept up by Thomas D'Arcy McGee's essay, 'A Plea for British American Nationality' in July 1863, followed by 'A Further Plea for a British American Nationality' in October. Indeed, McGee printed in the Magazine a 'card' saying he had intended to publish such a national magazine, but that he gladly left the task to Hind.[19]

How committed Hind was to the theme of nationality is revealed by an article he published in the *Canadian Journal* in November of 1863, entitled, 'A Glance at the Political and Commercial Importance of Central British America.' There was, he declared, no serious obstacle to communication between Lake Superior and Red River. As to the route over the prairies, he referred to the successful passage of the Overlanders of 1862. He argued the superior practicability of a Canadian railway and telegraph line over an American one. Paraphrasing or vaguely remembering the Speech from the Throne in 1858 to the British Parliament, he asserted that central British America was 'the key-stone of the arch' of 'a great Federation.' More important, 'in order to preserve our nationality in the face of the astonishing strides towards wealth and political importance ... [of] the United States, we must strengthen our position by extending British civilization where there is room for it to grow and expand.' The North was closed, the East occupied: '... the West alone remains to us.'[20]

A high note of nationalism was not the only feature of the *British American Magazine*, of course. It was eclectic in its choice of contents, perhaps because there was little choice. Hind himself published 'Sketches from Indian Life,' 'Salmon-spearing in Labrador by Torch Light,' 'On the Cultivation and Manufacture of Flax and Hemp in Canada,' and 'What is Spectrum Analysis?' - the last a fine example of his gift for clear and simple explanation.[21] The periodical lasted until April 1864, one full year.

There remains, however, the question of why at so opportune a time did Hind, the scientist and author, take up so strongly the role of nationalist and expansionist? An answer is suggested by his contacts with Edward Watkin during 1863.

The problem of expansion into the Northwest and the question of a federation of British North America were still very much alive, despite the depression. Even the replacement in May 1862 of the Cartier-Macdonald government - committed to federation if doubtful as to how western expansion was to be handled - by the economical ministry of John Sandfield Macdonald and Sicotte, did not end the pressures for both. The Duke of Newcastle kept working on a solution of the Hudson's Bay Company question, and the preparation of the Northwest for annexation to Canada, perhaps by making the Red River Settlement into a crown colony. The Grand Trunk Railway, which remained a liability to Canada and its stockholders, was interested. Its general manager, C.J. Brydges, saw a solution in expansion into the Maritimes, and worked for federation. Its new president, Edward Watkin, a forceful Victorian entrepreneur, saw the possibility of finding a new hinterland for the system by expansion, in cooperation with the Hudson's Bay Company, into the Northwest. This expansion was ensured by the firm financial base of the old company bought out by the International Finance Society in 1863 under Watkin's leadership, and the reorganization of the new company under Sir Edmund Head, late governor-general of Canada. Then Watkin came to Canada in July 1863 to explore the possibility of getting support from the government for a telegraph line to the Pacific.

Meanwhile early in 1863, the reluctant Canadian government, under Newcastle's prodding, considered resuming exploration in the Northwest. Hind, now definitely seeking full-time employment, perhaps sought to get an appointment on a survey. But the government drew back and the Inspector General of Revenue, Luther Holton, withdrew the estimate on the ground that no time remained for exploration in 1863.[22] It was then that Hind turned to Watkin.[23] On 25 March he wrote both privately and formally to Watkin in England to say he was interested in taking part in any development of the Northwest. He referred to passages in his *Report* of 1858 about the possibility of gold being found nearer Red River than the Rocky Mountains, and listed his experience and his publications, of which Watkins took note. He also gave his English references, including his being a Nottinghamshire man. Newcastle he had missed meeting while he was in Canada with the Prince of Wales in 1860, as he

himself was in England during the tour. But he
was, he wrote later, a friend of Colonel Sir
John Lefroy, late of the magnetic observatory
at Toronto, also of Mr. Digby Seymour, M.P. He
knew Lord Bury, Mr. Chichester Fortescue, friend
of Mr. Gladstone; Mr. Norton Shaw; and Lord
Frederick Cavendish, whom he had met in Red River
in 1858.[24]

It was quite an impressive introduction and,
when Watkin came to Canada, Hind got in touch
with him to find employment again in the Northwest
by making himself helpful to Watkin.[25] He pressed
on Watkin information received from Governor A.G.
Dallas of Rupert's Land of gold flakes being found
near Fort Ellice.[26] And he talked with Watkin's
knowledge to Gordon Brown of the *Globe*, to reassure
the latter that the newly reorganized company was
not asking all the lands of the Northwest for the
railway it was projecting, but only alternate ten
square miles.[27] He thought he had convinced Brown
that Watkin's enterprise would not harm Toronto's
interests in the Northwest and reported that the
people Brown spoke for asked only that the Canadian
tariff should be imposed to exclude American trade.
He was to see the great George Brown himself to
reduce the opposition to the railway project.[28]
Sometime, probably in August, he dined with Watkin,
McGee, Governor Dalls, Dr. Charles Mackay, who
had been correspondent of *The Times* for Canada,
and others at Niagara Falls.[29] Hind was now moving
in the circles of power, if only in the capacity
of publicist and agent. In September he informed
Watkin that the opposition in Toronto to the
Hudson's Bay Company and the Grand Trunk Railway,
consisting of certain parties of the 'old Northwest Navigation and Railway Company,' first formed
by William McDonell Dawson, were attempting to
frighten the Hudson's Bay Company into paying them
compensation for their rights. The attempt had come

to nothing, and Hind hoped the Hudson's Bay Company would proceed with a geological survey of the Northwest. He would like a post on such a survey. The cost would be about £2000, and he added there was hope of finding coal north of Riding Mountain. Meantime, he had had to apply for a post on the geological survey of Nova Scotia or of New Brunswick.[30]

Here then was sufficient reason, if not necessarily the only reason, for Hind's firm nationalism in 1863. He was hitching his own waggon, fairly enough, to the star of Canadian national destiny and seeking a new commission for exploration, to be followed, as he had told Watkin, by a survey of all British America.[31] It was the former Hind, but now in larger garments. One cannot help but admire the ambition of the still young man of thirty-nine.

It was his last effort, if not his last chance, to carry on the work of 1857 and 1858. Hind was not employed by Watkin. The Hudson's Bay Company's attempt to build the Pacific telegraph and railway twenty years before the Canadian Pacific Railway failed, and Hind's services, if ever wanted, were not needed. But he had definitely made up his mind to leave Trinity College, and had put out feelers in the Maritimes. Being denied in the west again, Hind had once more turned east.

VI Failure in New Brunswick 1864–1866

By the end of 1863 Hind had decided to leave Trinity College. His failure to gain fresh employment in the Northwest as an exponent of national expansion and an agent of Watkin in no way changed his determination to give up teaching. For the winter of 1863-64 he carried on as usual at Trinity, in the Royal Canadian Institute, and in his editorial duties. Then came an opportunity. He was invited to read a paper before the Royal Geological Society, and he went to England for that purpose in February 1864, apparently without formal leave from Trinity. His paper, published in the *Quarterly Journal* of the Geological Society, and republished in the *Canadian Journal* and the *Canadian Naturalist*,[1] was one of the best written and most scientific of his writings: 'Observations on Supposed Glacial Drift in the Labrador Peninsula, Western Canada, and on the South Branch of the Saskatchewan.' In it Hind relied on his own extensive observations to support Agassiz's theory of continental glaciation, as opposed to J.W. Dawson's hypothesis of land submergence and ice and water action on the lands submerged. If Hind is to be accepted at all as a geologist, it is on the basis of this paper and the quality of the observations from which it is drawn.

In itself, then, the visit to England in 1864 was a success. It was, however, more; it led to Hind's leaving Toronto. While in London he met the Hon. Peter Mitchell of New Brunswick, then a member of the government headed by S.L. Tilley. It is doubtful whether Hind had known Mitchell before, but the acquaintance, if it began in London in 1864, was twice to have important repercussions on Hind's life. It is probable that he approached Mitchell, first because Logan's aversion had closed the Geological Survey to him and the Northwest was quiescent, and also, because Nova Scotia and New Brunswick, following the recent gold strikes in the former province, were eager to have their geological resources surveyed. It was indeed a time of excitement in British North America, pumping oil in western Canada, mining gold on the Chaudière, gold in Nova Scotia, albertite in New Brunswick. A survey was the kind of activity Hind desired, and Mitchell, impressed by the chance to attract the services of a man of Hind's qualifications and public distinction, promised to recommend him to the government of New Brunswick for the post of provincial geologist.[2]

On the strength of this promise Hind visited Fredericton early in April, probably on his way back from England to Toronto. No doubt he met Mitchell and Tilley there. On 6 April he wrote a letter from Fredericton to Tilley, applying for the position of provincial geologist, stating his qualifications and giving his references. The latter were distinguished indeed, beginning with Sir Roderick Murchison, president of the Royal Geographical Society, but ending without Sir William Logan's name. He also listed his publications, and sent reviews, or extracts of reviews, of his *Narrative* and the *Labrador*. He ended by sketching a plan of the first year's work, at a cost of £1300. It was both an impressive and a characteristic document, well written, businesslike, with every advantage turned to the light and every disadvantage left in the shadow. It was even more in character that the forthcoming report was to be written up and published by the author.[3]

On 7 April Hind wrote a second letter, however, saying he had heard that only $500 had been appropriated for a geological survey. He would, he said, be prepared to make a preliminary survey for that sum of the rocks along the northern boundary of the province, the question of appointment as provincial geologist to lie by until the next year.[4] The sudden descent from $6500 to $500 is not explained; perhaps he had learned of opposition in the cabinet to an appointment. At any rate, the letter illustrates how determined Hind had become to leave Toronto and Canada, and find his own new field of geological work.

Perhaps it was also at this time that he met L.W. Bailey, professor of science at the University of New Brunswick. Young and ardent, a graduate of Harvard University, Bailey had already made a geological survey of part of New Brunswick in 1863, the expenses being paid by the lieutenant governor, Arthur Hamilton Gordon.[5] Bailey, despite the fact that he would have seemed to be the obvious man for the geological work now in view, welcomed Hind cordially, by his own account, and talked freely with him about the geology of the province. So did Bailey's collaborator, G.F. Matthew, an amateur geologist of distinction and a civil servant in Saint John, until he noted that, although Hind questioned and listened, he offered nothing of his own knowledge and experience.[6]

Tilley replied to Hind on 14 April, informing him that his offer of 7 April had been accepted by the Executive Council.[7] No sum was mentioned, no instructions were added to the brief, formal note, but apparently Hind was authorized to carry out a geological survey of the northern boundary of the province as he had indicated, and for the sum of $500. In the assembly the government's recommendation that Hind be authorized to begin the survey was at first rejected and then approved. Later, on 9 July, Hind's proposal of that date to extend the area of the survey was formally approved by the government.[8] Meanwhile, however, Tilley, so Bailey was to inform the provincial secretary's office, which was Tilley's department, in May 1865, orally instructed Bailey to continue in the southern counties the survey began in 1863, assuring him there was room for both surveys.[9] It was a decided preparation for misunderstanding and conflict, for which no explanation has yet emerged. No doubt there were good intentions all round; certainly both geologists acted in good faith.

It was, nevertheless, on an exceedingly slender basis indeed that Hind severed his ties with Trinity. Trinity was not at first ready to welcome him on his return from England. The Corporation resolved that no member of the faculty should take leave without their permission and their approval of the provision for his teaching during his absecne.[10] This annoyance passed, however, and when he resigned in May, the Corporation expressed regret and approved payment of his salary until 1 October.[11] Bishop Strachan in August wrote a general letter of recommendation, handsome if perhaps a trifle dry and rasping in its conclusion. As Hind was resigning to accept a post in New Brunswick, the bishop 'with pleasure and satisfaction' testified that he had been a good teacher, 'a gentleman of irreproachable character ... well known and much esteemed in this country who would be found a great acquisition in any seminary of learning as an able teacher in the Department of Science.' Further, Strachan went on, 'he has published several works of acknowledged merit and promises to rise to some distinction in the literary walk which he has chosen.'[12]

Hind had left Toronto late in May. From Montreal he wrote to Logan to request that specimens he collected might be examined by the Geological Survey, to which Logan assented as such co-operation with the other colonies had already been suggested by the Canadian government. Hind revealed in his letter to Logan that his purpose was to search for and examine in New Brunswick the rocks of the mineral-bearing 'Quebec group,' of the Eastern Townships of Canada. On 15 June Hind began his expedition at Dalhousie on the Bay of Chaleur, went to Campbellton on the Restigouche, ascended that river to the Upsalquitch, and descended the Nipisiquit to Bathurst. He had surveyed the outer limits of the Quebec Formation, now a major lead-zinc mining area. Prospects for mineral finds were so good that he went to Fredericton, and on 15 July received permission from Tilley to traverse the area. From Fredericton he went up the Saint John River to Woodstock and turned eastward overland to the southwest branch of the Miramichi at Boiestown. Returning to Woodstock, he went up the Tobique River as far as Gulquac, then came back to Little Falls towards the end of August before returning to Quebec.[13] In northern New Brunswick he encountered Sandford Fleming, who was making perliminary surveys for the Intercolonial Railway, and travelled with him by the Temiscouata route to the St. Lawrence. It was, of course, a meeting of friends, but Fleming does not indicate that the two were in any way collaborating.[14]

Hind had made a comprehensive survey of northern and central New Brunswick, another fine example of his powers as explorer and of his skill as a promoter of possibilities. Hind's and Fleming's parties emerged on the St. Lawrence River at Rivière du Loup, and went up the railway to Quebec. There Hind learned that the Canadian delegates to the Charlottetown Conference had left. Thus he had emerged from the forests of New Brunswick to enter the great current of Canadian life setting towards Confederation, the union of the provinces that was to open the Northwest, if not to Hind. Obviously in an attempt to keep his name to the forefront, he wrote Tilley at Charlottetown a preliminary report of the valuable possibilities he had detected on his survey.[15]

In September Hind settled his family in Fredericton and began, after some work in King's and Albert counties and on the Saint John River, to prepare his report. The stage was now being set for the 'Hind controversy' which was to stir the placidity of colonial Fredericton in the spring of 1865. While Hind had been surveying the Tobique River, Bailey with G.F. Matthew and H.C. Hartt, also an amateur geologist, was making a survey of the southern counties of the province. He too was preparing a report during the winter of 1864-65. Thus two geologists, one in the town by the broad river, one up the valley side in the gracious Georgian building of the university, were each writing a report, the printing of each to be paid for by one vote of $500. Hind had as yet no post and no settled income, and had moved his large family into a strange town. The two courses were set for collision.

It occurred when the reports were presented to the government in May 1865. Which one was to be printed? Hind, it is to be remembered, had undertaken to make a survey and submit a report for the whole sum of $500. The printing of Bailey's report along with other expenses was to cost $300 in the end, and in addition Tilley had authorized him at the end of 1864 to have 500 copies of a coloured geological map printed.[16] Further to complicate the issue, the government of Tilley had fallen in March, to be replaced by the anti-Confederation ministry of Albert J. Smith. While the scientists had been writing, the cause of Confederation had been defeated in the province. There was, therefore, no one left to assume the role Tilley would no doubt have played, of persuading the legislature that there was money to print two reports, he having said there was room for two surveys.

Certainly any government so disposed could have found the extra $300 even in New Brunswick in 1865. But it would seem from the testimony of L.W. Bailey, admittedly entirely one-sided and from a party to the dispute, but given over a number of years by a man of personal and scholarly integrity, and not given under pressure, that Hind may have behaved badly in the circumstances. When the legislature was confronted with the question of printing the two reports, *The Headquarters*, a local Fredericton daily, published on 10 May an editorial cruelly and even maliciously critical of Bailey's. Hind's report, it said, had been authorized by the late government, Bailey's by the late assembly. (The latter statement, in view of Tilley's own authorization of Bailey's work, was not wholly correct.) The authors of the Bailey report, the editorial went on, presumed to attempt to rewrite the geology of New Brunswick, already outlined by Abraham Gesner when provincial geologist and Dr. James Robb, late professor of natural history in the University of New Brunswick. In particular, they had arrogantly and to no purpose changed the geological nomenclature introduced by Robb. Bailey's report did indeed introduce such changes, and it was indeed a reworking of Robb's earlier work. The changes were not unreasonable ones and an intensification of geological work in the province was necessary, despite the pioneering work of Robb.

Bailey, in a reply over his own signature, made this defence and added that Principal J.W. Dawson of McGill, author of *Acadian Geology*, had approved his report. But what was objectionable in the editorial was its bitter, almost vicious, tone of disparagement of men alleged to be youthful and amateur upstarts. Who wrote it under the cover of the editorial 'We'?

Bailey then believed firmly, and continued to believe until the end of his life, that Hind had written the anonymous editorial.[17] There is no evidence known to the writer, and none was supplied by Bailey, that Hind either wrote or inspired the editorial. As far as documentation goes, there the matter must rest for the moment. But Bailey was an unimpeachable witness, one who had the grace to request a later inquirer into the matter, W.F. Ganong, 'to make allowances for the exaggeration and too exalted imagination of early youth.'[18] It is true also that Hind's position was precarious, and that he had staked everything on a position promised by one member of a government, which had then fallen. Moreover, he evidently thought, if incorrectly, that Bailey and Matthew were opposing his appointment as provincial geologist. They had in fact told Tilley they would stand aside in favour of Hind, but Tilley had waved aside their generous offer.[19] In what was anger, or even panic, Hind may have used means of defence which, if they may be extenuated, cannot be excused.

The controversy had broken. Bailey's reply on 17 May over his signature in *The Headquarters* brought it out into the open. Other papers took up the theme, some approving Hind's report, others Bailey's, but really not in a partisan spirit.[20] It was in the Assembly that there was difficulty, and perhaps not just partisan strife but conflict between the North Shore and Saint John Valley members. The relevant papers were called for on 1 May, and duly tabled.[21] In the upshot the matter was smoothed over; both reports were printed and became part of the geological literature of New Brunswick.[22]

It was, nevertheless, only the public controversy that was ended. The more serious conflict was partly scientific, even more professional, and perhaps personal. Hind, with his usual expansiveness, had made his report cover much more than the area he had surveyed. He clearly intended that it would demonstrate his fitness to be provincial geologist. It discussed, for example, the peculiar mineral deposit, albertite, found in Albert County in the south, and mined for refining as illuminating gas. He gave as his opinion that albertite was probably fossilized, or 'inspissated,' petroleum.[23] J.W. Dawson agreed with him, as Bailey was later to do, but the latter had already committed himself to the opinion that it was a rarefied form of a highly bituminous coal. The subject was much debated, because the striking of petroleum in Canada West in 1857 and in Pennsylvania in 1859 had raised Maritime interest in the possibility of oil in the same geological formations. Drilling for oil had begun in the province in 1864. If albertite were a product of petroleum, then liquid petroleum might be found where it occurred. This controversy was, however, a fair difference of opinion and Hind had the better of it.

The deeper conflict really arose from the distrust of Hind which both Bailey and Matthew had formed when they welcomed him to New Brunswick in 1864. When they read his *Preliminary Report on the Geology of New Brunswick*, it confirmed their distrust. Hind, they were certain, had used their ideas and their material in his report without due acknowledgment. Their view of it was contained in, even perhaps expressed by one of them in, an anonymous review in the *American Journal*. 'This Report is made up, partly from the author's observations and largely from other sources.'[24] In short, they thought and continued to think thereafter that Hind was a plagiarist.[25]

It is a subtle point. Hind did freely use, in all his reports, other scientists' material, more than the sensitivity of eager scholars could apparently accept. He did, however, conscientiously give his sources and make clear when he quoted. He did not, however, use other people's ideas and materials to support his own arguments or to refute theirs; that is, his use was not the employment of others' work in the manner proper to critical scholarship. He used their material in the large to fill out his own writing, and, even with credit given, in effect published it as his own. His was an open plagiarism, but none the less plagiarism, the theft of other people's words and ideas.

From suspicion on this score Hind never freed himself in the minds of Bailey and Matthew, nor in that of Sir William Logan.[26] On the other hand, Hind retained the friendship of Sandford Fleming, and seems always to have enjoyed the respect of J.W. Dawson.[27] It is not therefore for the author of this study to cast up any final account. What it does seem pertinent to say is that Hind can be criticized in two major respects. One is that he used the material of others not just for reference or in criticism, but for description and for the rounding out of reports that went beyond his own observations. In doing so, he followed the practice of many in his field, notably the famous geologist Charles Lyell; Hind, nevertheless unlike Lyell, revealed himself as not a scholar, but, for want of a better term, what may be called a publicist. He also demonstrated that he was not a severely trained and professional scientist; he was not a geologist, but a geological surveyor and a descriptive writer, talented in the kind, but no more.

It is possible, however, to be too severe in judging Hind, as it would seem Bailey and Logan were. A reputable geologist, R.W. Ells of the Geological Survey of Canada, could in the lifetime of both Bailey and Hind acknowledge the value of, and even commend certain aspects of, Hind's *Preliminary Report*. It is apparent from Ells's remarks that Hind contributed significantly both to the difficult task of defining the geological formation of New Brunswick and to the over all survey of the geology of the province.[28] And it is apparent in general that he did establish the nature of albertite, and that the criticism, whether his or not, of the novel nomenclature of Bailey and Matthew was justified. His basic competence as a geologist, if limited, could not be questioned. Ells makes it evident that his remarks were in part an attempt to strike a balance between parties each to a degree right in their contentions.

Hind in addition had a flair he could not control; he always used any geological evidence, lignite on the Souris, crystalline limestone on the Shield, albertite in New Brunswick, to suggest economic possibilities in an exciting way far beyond the bounds of scientific prudence. Even the one scientific finding of his *Preliminary Report* - that there were 'Quebec group,' that is metalliferous, rocks, in central northern New Brunswick,[29] had an economic bearing. It is a difficulty all geologists face, as Logan had done in the survey every year and in every chapter of the *Geology of Canada*. But Logan always kept within the bounds of scientific discretion; the whole of the *Geology* is rigidly scientific, except for one chapter on 'Economic Geology' in which economic possibilities are soberly assessed.[30] Hind was ever the promoter, however, the seeker after new frontiers. There was always gold in any hills he traversed.

The Hind controversy, then, had in the upshot two consequences: a serious loss of reputation for Hind among workers in the same field, a loss further to that already incurred by his reports on the Northwest, and the end of his hope of becoming the provincial geologist of New Brunswick. It is true, of course, that he might not have received that appointment in any event. The new government was not bound by the intentions of the old; the upset of the movement towards Confederation may have distracted attention from geological explorations, at least for the moment. Yet it is to be noted that Hind perhaps stood well with Smith, who was to accept him for an important appointment in 1877.[31]

Hind also, it would appear, did not give up hope. He remained with his family in Fredericton through the winter of 1865-66, and wrote a pamphlet entitled *Resources of the Province of New Brunswick*, a description of the agriculture of the province. He made an excursion to the coal fields of Cape Breton.[32] In July of 1865 tragedy struck. His eldest son, Frank, aged sixteen, drowned while bathing in the Saint John River.[33]

Whether that loss precipitated the decision to give up the hope of an appointment in New Brunswick cannot be known. We do know that Hind wrote to Joseph Henry, secretary of the Smithsonian Institution, to say he had decided to become a 'Consulting Geologist' and he asked to be recommended for work in the United States. Then, in the fall of 1866, he took up residence in Windsor, Nova Scotia, choosing it because of King's College, the Anglican church school and university college, where his children could be educated. Undoubtedly the geological activity in Nova Scotia also attracted him as a field for private undertakings.

Hope of a public appointment he could not have; Nova Scotia had a provincial geologist, the Rev. Dr. D. Honeyman, and King's College had a professor of chemistry, the Rev. Henry How.[34] The beauty of the Windsor district must too have appealed to Hind, with his vivid love of landscape.

In Windsor he took up his residence, for whatever complex of reasons, and it was to be his home until his death. That the principal reason was the education and security of his family is to be inferred from two deeds executed to make a home in Windsor possible, On 25 September 1865, Hind and Mrs. Hind made his brother, James Fisher Hind of New York, described as 'Gentleman, of that city,' trustee for Mrs. Hind for land or money inherited from her father in Canada and for her expectations of inheriting from Miss Caroline Back of Bath. James was to administer her estate 'in trust in the public funds of Nova Scotia or the British North American province, or in real estate.' If James were to die before Mrs. Hind, she was to be free to will her property 'without permission of her present or any future husband.' The Hinds were a loving couple, but clearly Mrs. Hind was to be free to look after the family no matter what future adventures Hind undertook or what disasters he incurred.[35]

James then bought on 2 October 1866, from Benjamin Weir, a Halifax banker, two lots of land in Windsor on the main road to Halifax. One lot, with a house, was known as 'Sunnyside.' The other lay between Sunnyside and 'the old burying ground,' of which Hind was to write the history, and across the road from Maplewood cemetery. The two comprised an area of two chains frontage by three chains depth, enough to pasture a horse and cow at least, and leave room for an ample garden. The price was $7,000 Nova Scotia currency, Weir taking a mortgage of $5500 at 6 per cent interest to be paid off in five years in two payments a year. Mrs. Hind and James, not Henry Youle, signed both documents.[36] On Sunnyside a spacious wooden house was built, and there the family, or some members of it, lived until 1941.

VII The Last Controversy and the Long Peace

At Sunnyside, just outside Windsor, the affectionate family life of the Hinds continued, its happiness broken only by the deaths of two other sons: James Archibald, who died of unknown causes after the Hinds came to Windsor, and John Youle who died of typhoid in 1880.[1] His older boys, Duncan Henry and Kenneth Cameron, went to King's College, his two daughters, Katherine Sarah and Margaret Jane, in due course to the new girls' school of Edgehill. It is important to remember that Hind's life, often so contentious and stormy, was at its centre as sunny and peaceful as a summer forest glade.

King's College was to become the focus of Hind's public existence in his last years. Church of England, it was the Nova Scotian counterpart of Trinity College in Toronto. As a place of education for his children, it was thus most acceptable to Hind. He was, however, never to repeat that part of his Toronto life furnished by Trinity College. With the business community of Windsor, on the other hand, he found awaiting him a role he had played in Toronto. He became in Windsor as in Toronto a professional prospector, a seeker after possibilities of expansion and development. Windsor had, like Toronto, a small, aggressive circle of businessmen ready to exploit the primary resources of the surrounding country. In 1872 they were to form the Mineral Exploration and Mining Association of Nova Scotia,[2] the president and one other director being on the board of King's College. Hind was exactly the man they needed. The years 1869 to 1873 were in fact to give Hind a second career and prove his most prolific years in the production of pamphlets on resources, particularly mining resources. He was to appear fully as a promoter in the publication of the last of this group, *A Forecast of the Future of the Maritime Provinces* (1876).[3]

The provincial government of Nova Scotia also welcomed Hind. It was eager to continue the search for minerals begun after 1867 in order to help repair the loss of revenue caused by Confederation. Hind was therefore retained by the commissioner of mines to make a number of surveys in districts of possible interest for gold or coal, which he did with his usual acute sense of possibilities, and with considerable professional skill.[4] Hind thus found plentiful occasion to act as 'a consulting geologist.' Also, because of Fleming's continuing friendship while he supervised the building of the Intercolonial until 1876, Hind became involved with him and Charles Tupper in the development of the Spring Hill coalfields north of Windsor. Through this enterprise he also developed an interest with John Kelly, deputy commissioner of mines, in the railway from Parrsboro to Spring Hill across the basin from Windsor.

Hind in these years had some speculative interest in his own professional work. He was never, in part in consequence, to be employed by the Geological Survey of Canada when it came into Nova Scotia after Confederation. It gave the Rev. D. Honeyman, the former provincial geologist, special assignments, but Hind, towards whom Logan had become bitterly hostile, was ignored because Logan believed that he was suspected of having an interest in certain gold mines.[5] The provincial government, however, was happy enough to employ a man of Hind's undoubted professional reputation. At the same time Hind was able to continue his own free-lance work. In the 1870s he also became a valued correspondent of the Smithsonian Institution, as a fair amount of correspondence attests.

Nothing Hind did in Nova Scotia furnished a basis for another large publication such as the *Narrative* or the *Labrador*. He did, however, prepare a paper read in London in April 1870 before the Geological Society and also the Society of Arts: 'On Two Gneissoid Series in Nova Scotia and New Brunswick.' It was an extension of the claim of his *Preliminary Report* to have found a 'Quebec group' formation in New Brunswick. He now argued that the group also appeared in Nova Scotia and that the two series were equivalent to the Huronian and Laurentian rocks of Canada. It was, further study was to prove, an incorrect argument, but Principal Dawson of McGill was present and supported Hind, as did a Mr. Henry Robinson who had been with Hind in the Nova Scotia goldfields.[6]

The article was at least a good scientific venture, as its publication in *Nature* and in the *Quarterly Journal* of the Geological Society demonstrated. He reworked the same theme in an article 'On the Laurentian and Huronian Series in Nova Scotia' in the *American Journal* (1874), apparently his only publication in an American scientific journal. The inevitable Hind touch came in the conclusion that, if his argument were sound, the existence of these formations would be of 'considerable economic advantage to the province.' Hind could not long continue to be the pure scientist.

In a paper published in *Nature* in 1874, however, he was just that. 'The Figure of the Earth in

Relation to Geological Inquiry,' discusses the imperfect rotundity of the globe, and offers mathematical descriptions of the imperfections. These, he suggested, were to be explained by a theory of globular undulation. He reasoned from the evidences of change in the levels of seas and lakes and, with an irrepressible Hind touch, alluded to 'the stupendous escarpments which for 1,000 to 1,700 miles rear their wall-like fronts from 200 to 600 feet above the Ontario, Red River and Saskatchewan plains.'[7] Hind, as always, could turn a phrase if not launch a geological theory.

In 1876, when the mining boom in Nova Scotia was unfortunately over, came a fresh opportunity in a new area, an invitation from a Nova Scotia friend of German birth, Francis von Ellerhausen, to make a geological survey in Labrador. Nothing is known of the reasons for the expedition except that Ellerhausen was proprietor of the Betts Cove Copper Mine in Newfoundland.[8] The voyage was to give a new and drastic turn to Hind's career.

It almost failed, however, to take place, for when Hind was about to leave in early May 1876 he received from Sandford Fleming a proposal that he might make a journey along the proposed route of the Canadian Pacific Railway and write a volume or two on the subject. Hind replied to say he was ready to do so, if his terms were met, and if he heard from Fleming before he took ship for his voyage. He did not, and the incident is of interest only because it reveals the still continuing friendship of the men, and gives another example of Hind's technique of exploration, report, and published narrative. In his reply to Fleming he suggested a title for the proposed work, 'The Zone of the Canadian Pacific Railway,' which, he commented, 'sounds and looks and reads well - as good as 'Fertile Belt.'[9] The report was perhaps intended by Fleming to affect the dispute over the route in

British Columbia, which was to lead to Fleming's withdrawal as engineer-in-chief of the surveys in 1880.

Hind thus spent the summer of 1876 on the coast of Labrador, going as far as 350 miles north of the Straits of Belle Isle. From this expedition came some further geological observations on the great peninsula, reported in his 'Notes on Some Geological Features of the North Eastern Coast of Labrador,' a further discovery of crystalline limestone, and his 'Notes on the Fishing Grounds of Northern Labrador,' a description of new submarine banks Newfoundland fishermen were beginning to exploit. Hind also became deeply interested in the action of ice and ocean currents. The total result was another outpouring of his fertile mind. In 1877 he prepared a number of articles as a result of the voyage.[10] In 1878 he displayed at the Universal Exhibition in Paris a map of the oceanic currents of the region which was awarded a gold medal and diploma.[11] Hind also tried once more to make a book of his work in Labrador and on the fisheries. He offered his manuscript to Macmillan, London, but that firm of publishers rejected it on the ground that they did not wish to deal with one of Messrs. Longmans clients.[12] It was a defeat of his final effort to repeat his formula of reports of exploration published as a book, and shows him to be still the active, venturesome Hind. New fields, new subjects, always called out the native talent of the bright boy of William Butler's school. And in 1877 the voyage led to an invitation from the government of Newfoundland, perhaps suggested by Fleming, then railway consultant on the island, to undertake a geological survey in that colony.

The Labrador venture, however, was to have another and more far-reaching consequence. The Treaty of Washington of 1871 had provided by Article XXI for an award by arbitration of compensation for any losses Canadian fishermen might suffer under the terms of the treaty, which admitted American fishermen to Canadian waters. A duly constituted commission, consisting of one American representative, E.H. Kellogg, one British, Hon. A.T. Galt, and one neutral jointly agreed on, Baron Delfosse of Belgium, met in Halifax in June 1877 to hold hearings to decide what the losses might have been. Hon. A.J. Smith, Canada's minister of fisheries, suggested that Hind should appear before the commission as a representative of Newfoundland.[13] Hind duly prepared a submission on *The Effect of the Fisheries Clauses of the Treaty of Washington on the Fishers and Fisheries of British North America*, which he published with his 'Notes on the Fishing Grounds of Northern Labrador' as an addendum.[14] One of the best pieces of work Hind had done, it is also another example of his private publication of an official document. He was examined in person before the commission, and the American counsel tried to discredit him by asking if he had not certified some Nova Scotian gold stocks in Boston. Hind angrily denied that he had. His competence as a witness was also questioned, and Hind in reply twice asserted that he was 'by profession a geologist.'[15]

He suffered no discredit because of this rough handling, and indeed became curator of the papers of the commission with the task of putting them in order.[16] In the session of the Parliament of Canada in 1878 he was called to give expert testimony before a committee of the House of Commons. He stated his opinion, in view of his experience in Labrador, that the Hudson Bay route might be used to open and settle the Northwest with emigrants from Britain. He was again the far-seeing promoter, pushing hastily assembled scientific evidence to far lengths to promote a policy.[17]

Both subjects, the fisheries and the settlement of the Northwest, by a sudden outburst on Hind's part, were to run together and involve him in a campaign which he was to press with all his strength and which was to take all his time from 1878 to 1883. These years make up a most curious and largely inexplicable chapter of Hind's life, which only exhaustive research and much more space could set out with any hope of full explanation.

The affair began with an accusation by Hind that the officials of the Canadian government had falsified the fisheries statistics on which the Halifax Award of 1877 had been based. Those alleged to be guilty were Sir Albert Smith, former minister of fisheries; W.F. Whitcher, commissioner of fisheries; and Edward Young, Canadian-born director of the Bureau of Statistics of the United States and a relative of Sir Albert. The attack, repeated in letter after letter to the press, together with letters to Prime Minister Gladstone, Lord Frederick Cavendish, President Grant of the United States, and others, was followed by the allegation that the prospects of land settlement in the Northwest had been fraudently misrepresented by members of the Geological Survey of Canada and the Canadian Pacific Railway Company to sell the stocks of the latter and justify the change of route from the northern parkland to the southern prairies. The two 'Charges' became an indictment for a conspiracy begun with the purchase of the rights of the Hudson's Bay Company for Canada in 1870, carried on in the Treaty of Washington, 1871, in the Fisheries Award of 1877, in the sale of Canadian Pacific stock and lands after 1880, and finally in the surveys of the southern prairies by John Macoun for the Geological Survey in 1880 and 1881. Hind termed Macoun in public print 'a charlatan.' The men Hind cited as involved ranged from the

Earl of Kimberley, governor of the Hudson's Bay Company until 1868, and Sir Stafford Northcote, his successor, through many others, but above all W.F. Whitcher, Macdonald's adviser on the fisheries at Washington in 1871, commissioner of fisheries in the department, and secretary to the royal commission on the construction of the Canadian Pacific Railway in 1879, and finally, ever and always, Sir Alexander T. Galt. The core of the Charges was that the funds gained by the sale of the Hudson's Bay Territory and the Fisheries Award were being used to finance the Canadian Pacific Railway and to settle the Northwest in an area where death and mutilation by drought and frost awaited the misinformed immigrant. It was a sustained and sweeping philippic for which no motive is evident, except Hind's own claim to zeal in the public cause.

The years 1878 to 1883 thus saw a prodigious effort by Hind, ending in the fevered language of his *An Exposition of the Fisheries Commission Frauds, showing how the frauds were concealed by the use of the number 666 and the masking numbers 42, 10, 7, 2, taken from the 13th Chapter of Revelation.* Such a device would be as good as another, but clearly Hind had passed the limits of sobriety.

It is, however, unprofitable for want of any evidence of Hind's motives to follow the details of Hind's labyrinthine development of the Charges from 1878 to 1883. For an understanding of the man himself it is perhaps enough to say that he drove them to a pitch far beyond the borders of libel with a view to forcing a public hearing in the expectation of proving them. The Charges were largely ignored, except for some discussion in the press and in Parliament and Congress. A few thought he had been and would be, in Macdonald's phrase, a 'troublesome and mischief-making person'; another called him 'a ruffian'; one journalist compared him with an assassin; no one answered him.[18]

Prime Minister Macdonald did have W.F. Whitcher prepare a memorandum to refute Hind's accusations.[19] The general attitude towards them was that, in Galt's words, they had not 'excited much attention for the reason that no one believes them.'[20] Sir Charles Dilke said in the British House of Commons that they were 'groundless and incredible.'[21] Hind's effort had only brought down on his head a biting silent scorn. Sandford Fleming and some others might stand by him in private,[22] but in public he was left isolate.

Yet Dilke's comment was, in fact, not entirely true. There were errors in the fisheries statistics, and good grounds to think the Halifax Award excessive, as Spencer Baird of the Smithsonian Institution assured Hind he was 'fully satisfied.' Edward Young was dismissed, perhaps coincidentally, from the United States Bureau of Statistics. The award sat unused in the Public Accounts of Canada from 1879 to 1883. The choice of the southern route for the Canadian Pacific did increase the difficulties of settlement inherent in the climate of the Northwest. What really was, and remains, incredible was Hind's crowning charge that leading statesmen and businessmen in Great Britain and Canada had 'conspired' to bring about the purchase of the Hudson's Bay Company's rights in the Northwest, and doctor the fishing statistics in order to enlarge the Halifax Award that they might acquire the funds to build the Pacific railway.[23]

This was surely frenzy. Hind was right to protest about the fisheries statistics when convinced there was fraud, even if, as must be assumed, he was in error. And in the matter of the settlement of the southern prairies, at that date at least, he was largely right. But his persistence, his cantankerousness, his complete lack of generosity or feeling for those he denounced in wildly libellous language, put him and left him quite out of court. Hind was accusing others, as it were, of what he had himself been accused of, fraud, plagiarism, appropriation of others' work. The result was that he contradicted and destroyed himself professionally. The scientist became the polemicist, the promoter the anti-promoter, the publicist the fantasticist. Hind may have received money from parties opposed to the Canadian Pacific Railway for making and pressing his charges, but no evidence has been found. What seems morally certain is that his character, his frustration, and his sense of failure and of talents unrecognized are in themselves sufficient explanation.

What perhaps can be said is that the five-year controversy was at bottom a fierce expression of long-suppressed frustrations. He had failed to be taken on by the Geological Survey; he had failed repeatedly to find a means of return to the Northwest; he had failed to publish a book on the fisheries. The proud, withdrawn, always bright boy, still apparent in the thrusting, hawk-like countenance of the older Hind, who remained conscious of his undoubted talents, was making one last frantic demonstration of his prowess, attacking the civil servants, the politicians, the businessmen, finally even the sacred Survey itself, all the men and circumstances that seemed to have denied a clear run to his talents.

It was the climacteric of his life. Thereafter, from 1884 to his death in 1908, Hind wrote no more on any scientific or public subject. Why can only be guessed. He spent the last quarter-century of his life in the peace of Windsor and his family life at Sunnyside. That he was able to do so and be remembered as a reserved but kindly man,[24] reveals that the charges he had incurred and the controversies he had aroused left no scar on mind or conscience. Hind, it may now be said, was no deliberate plagiarist; he was not a designing fomenter of controversies created for personal advantage; he was a self-taught scientist who felt that science was an enterprise in which all might engage freely and even for profit. He saw no reason to forgo its obvious utility; he clearly believed that he who got first to market was entitled to sell his findings. He thus failed to be a professional scientist of Logan's standard; he became a practising geological surveyor who sold his services to any employer; he was at his best in the freest of all scientific pursuits, the broad, quick exploratory survey. The summers on the Assiniboine and Saskatchewan remained the summit of his career.

In final appraisal of that career it seems best to see Hind not as a scientist or even as a publicist, but as an active and even distinguished member of the group of men gathered in the Royal Canadian Institute, a group peculiar to its time, who brought personal talents and varied training to tasks now discharged by specialists. As such a man, Hind achieved much. He was the surveyor, the explorer, the advocate of possibilities sensed rather than defined, one of those once called trail-breakers or even makers of nations. He helped to open the Northwest, itself a considerable achievement for any man.

After 1883, Hind remained what he had always been, a man sure of himself and lovable to those he loved. His family life continued gentle and happy; the one loss was the death of his mother in Nottingham[25] in 1884, which meant the end of the old connection with England. King's College became the central interest of his declining years, and especially the history of the college and of his neighbourhood. In 1889 he published a pleasantly written history of the Old Burying Ground of Windsor, which lay untended by his own lot. In 1890 came his *Centennial History of ... King"s*

College, on which he did considerable research and for which, with his other services as a member of the board, he was awarded a D.C.L. by King's that year.[26]

One could wish that on such a minor note Hind's career had ended. But his service on the board from 1886 to 1887 brought him into contact with Mr. F.C. Sumichrast, proprietor and headmaster of 'Girton House, Boarding and Day School for Young Ladies' in Halifax. The young ladies were for the most part clergymen's daughters.[27] Nothing is known of the personal relations of the two men, but Hind's strong sense of righteousness was to lead him into another, the last, of his controversies. He wrote to Bishop Hibbert Binney of Nova Scotia to inform him he had learned that, before coming to Canada, Sumichrast had divorced his wife.[28] In Nova Scotia, while his first wife was still living, he had married again, something very necessary for the head of a girls' school, but, in the circumstances, against the canons of the Church of England.

Hind, it may be held, did no more than was necessary in telling the bishop of what he had discovered. Sumichrast, however, learned of what Hind had done, and laid suit for libel with damages of $20,000. The case was first on the docket of the Nova Scotia Supreme Court of 27 May 1887. The hearing was anticipated with considerable interest by the press and public, the more so as Alexander Graham Bell, the inventor of the telephone, was a personal friend of Sumichrast from college days in Scotland. He and Sumichrast, known in Scotland as Roussy, had come to America in 1870. Bell now hurried up from Washington to bear witness to his friend's character. The case, however, was never heard. It was settled out of court by the church dignitaries on Hind's agreeing to pay $1,500 damages.[29] There was talk of pursuing the matter in the ecclesiastical court; nothing was done. But Girton House closed, Sumichrast left Halifax, and there was no school for Anglican young ladies in Nova Scotia.

Post hoc but not necessarily *propter hoc* with respect to Hind, the resulting vacuum was filled by the creation, on the initiative of the alumni of King's, of Edgehill School for Girls. It was to stand on the same spur of rising ground on which King's stood, overlooking Windsor on one side and Hind's Sunnyside on the other. The school opened in 1890, with Hind as secretary of its trustees and secretary of its board.[30] Edgehill flourished from that day to this and Hind remained as secretary, then managing director, until his death in 1908. So closely was he identified with it that in one of his obituaries he was even called 'President' of Edgehill.[31] He had found an occupation for the last eighteen years of his life, and the school, clearly, was very much his creation. Some remnants of his own library are still on the shelves of the school's library, great names being among the authors, von Humboldt, Maury, Agassiz.[32]

In the annual routine of the school, then, and the placid tenor of the Windsor countryside, with the tides of Fundy filling and draining the broad throat of the Avon, with wide meadows and dark oak clumps reaching out to the enclosing hills, Hind lived out the peaceful close of a strenuous career that had led him from Nottingham to Toronto, from Louisiana to Labrador, from the headwaters of the Qu'Appelle to those of the Moisie. He is still remembered at Windsor as a reserved and gentle old man who always had daily crumbs for the sparrows on the verandah at Sunnyside and apples from his orchard for the children straying home from school.

In February 1906 he was weakened by an attack of *la grippe*, but not until July 1908, when he was in his 86th year, did he take to his bed. He died on 8 August, and was buried in Maplewood where his family, except for his two surviving sons, and including the faithful English nanny, Jenny Walker, and errant brother William, the artist, are now assembled.[33] Hind's personal effects consisted of an estate of $2,680 in bank shares, his books, some farm produce, two cows, and one old horse 'of no value.'[34] His collection of Western Canadiana was dispersed at that time. His especially loved daughter, Margaret, moved into Sunnyside after her mother's death; his daughter Katherine and her husband lived there until her death in 1941, when Sunnyside was sold out of the family.[35]

Hind was not wholly forgotten. *Science* carried a brief factual obituary. His northwestern explorations had been noticed with respect in the standard *Geography of North America* by F.V. Hayden, chief of the U.S. Geological Survey, and A.R.C. Selwyn, director of the Geological Survey of Canada, published in, of all years, 1883. As late as 1915 his Labrador explorations were noted in H.M. Ami's *Canada and the United States*.[36] His *Narrative*, even his *Labrador*, are still read and sought after by bibliophiles, and will be as long as the history of exploration and of the Northwest draws men as both drew Hind.

Notes

CHAPTER ONE
1. G.M. Rose (ed.), *A Cyclopaedia of Canadian Biography, Being Chiefly Men of the Time* ..., II (Toronto, 1888), pp. 308-309, the most detailed of the biographical articles on Hind; County Archives, Nottinghamshire, Parish Register, St. Mary's Church Nottingham, No. 587.
2. Public Reference Library, Nottingham Archives, Apprentice Files, 1821.
3. British Association for the Advancement of Science, 1937, 'Introduction,' *History of Nottingham*, p. 103; H.Y. Hind, *Narrative of ... Red River ... and of ... Saskatchewan Exploring Expedition* (London, 1860), II, 37.
4. So my researches in archives and directories revealed; Duncan Gray, in *Nottingham through Five Hundred Years: A History of Town Government* (Nottingham, 1968), p. 68, notes that 'Hynde' was a local name from the seventeenth century.
5. Public Reference Library, Nottingham Archives, Thomas Hind to his solicitor 19 June 1815, from London, letter franked by J.W. Croker, Secretary of the Admiralty.
6. The Parish Register of St. Mary's at the time of Henry Youle's christening gives Thomas Hind's

address as St. Mary's Gate, and in D.E. Varley's *A History of the Midland Counties Lace Manufacturers' Association, 1815-1958* (Long Eaton, 1959), p. 89, he is described as 'an important person in the warp lace and bobbin net trade.' See also Ronald S. Walton, *The History of the Nottingham Chamber of Commerce, 1860-1960* (Nottingham, 1961), pp. 17-18.

7 William White, *History, Gazetteer and Directory of Nottinghamshire, 1832* (Nottingham, 1832), p. 258; Public Reference Library, Nottingham Archives, extracts of will of George Youle, 1849, leaving 1/7 of residue of his estate to his sister, Sarah Youle Hind, and to her children. By an indenture to the will it appears the 1/7 of the residue was settled in 1850 for £700 of Midland Railway Stock.

8 Roy A. Church in his *Economic and Social Change in a Midland Town: Victorian Nottingham, 1815-1900* (London, 1966), p. 12; also S.D. Chapman, 'Working-Class Housing in Nottingham during the Industrial Revolution,' *Transactions of the Thoroton Society* (Nottingham), LXVII (1963), 83.

9 J.D. Chambers, 'Nottingham in the Early Nineteenth Century,' *TTS*, XLIV (1941), 40.

10 J.D. Chambers, 'Nottingham in the Early Nineteenth Century,' *TTS*, XLVII (1943), 29-40.

11 J.D. Chambers, 'Victorian Nottingham,' *TTS*, LXIII (1959), 6.

12 Searches both by the author and by Mr. W. David Crane of Nottingham have failed to discover any record of a will by Thomas Hind. In the Public Library, Nottingham Archives, is a reference to the death of a Thomas Hind, 25 March 1845. I owe this information to the kindness of Mr. Crane.

13 Information about the school comes from A.W. Thomas, *A History of Nottingham High School* (Nottingham, 1957), pp. 132, 139-144.

14 W.R. Stevenson, 'Nottingham High School Fifty

Years Ago,' *The Forester* (Nottingham), July 1887.
15 *White's Directory*, 1844 and 1853, notes Thomas Hind as 'bank clerk,' and Mr. Crane identified the bank for the author as the Nottingham Savings Bank.
16 F. Paulsen (tr. T. Lorenz), *German Education Past and Present* (London, 1908), pp. iv and 66; W.H.R.A. Lexis, comp., *Das Unterrichtswesen im Deutschen Reich; aus Anlass der Weltausstellung in St. Louis unter Mitwirkung zahlreicher Fachmänner* (Berlin, 1904), p. 195; Friedrich Paulsen, *Geschichte des gelehrten Unterrichts auf den deutschen Schulen und Universitäten vom Ausgang des Mittelalters bis zur Gegenwart* (Leipzig, 1885), p. 642; Fritz W. Neefe, *Geschichte der Leipziger Allegemeinen Zeitung, 1837-1843* (Leipzig, 1914).
17 F.E. Farrington, *Commercial Education in Germany* (New York, 1914), pp. 171-195; Otto Kaemmel, *Geschichte des Leipziger Schulwesens vom Anfange des 13. bis gegen die mitte des 19. Jahrhunderts (1214-1846)* (Leipzig, Berlin, 1909).
18 This is a conjecture, based to a degree on Hind's possession in his library of Humboldt's *Cosmos: A Sketch of a Physical Description of the Universe*, 4 vols., and the passing quotations from his works, but mostly on Hind's outlook on natural science and his style in describing natural phenomena.
19 Rose, *Cyclopaedia*, II, 308.
20 J.A. Vann, *Alumni Cantabrigienses*, Part II, vol. III, 1752-1900 (Cambridge, 1947), p. 379.
21 Rose, *Cyclopaedia*, II, 308.
William Logan Papers, Hind to Logan, 3 July 1857.
22 McCord Museum, Logan Papers, Hind to Logan, 3 July 1857; also Appleton, *Cyclopedia of American Biography*, vol. 3 (New York, 1887).
23 *Canadian Journal*, I (1) August 1852, p. 26,

reference to Hind's article, source not given.
24 C.B. Sissons, *Egerton Ryerson: His Life and Letters* (Toronto, 1947), I, 154.

CHAPTER II
1 For references to the opening of the Normal School, see Thomas Kirkland, 'Brief Sketch of the Toronto Normal School,' *The Toronto Normal School, 1847-1897, Jubilee Celebration* (Toronto, 1898), pp. 23, 41-47; C.B. Sissons, *Egerton Ryerson: His Life and Letters* (Toronto, 1947), II, 149, fn. 2.
2 Kirkland, 'Toronto Normal School,' p. 24; *British Colonist*, Nov. 2 and 9, 1847, cited by Kirkland, p. 24; *Globe*, 3 Nov. 1847; J.G. Hodgins, *Documentary History of Education in Ontario*, VII (Toronto, 1900), 97-101.
3 Sissons, *Ryerson*, II, 230, fn. 1.
4 *Ibid.*, p. 230.
5 Rose, *Cyclopaedia*, II, 309.
6 Roswell's *Toronto Directory*, 1850, p. 61; Brown's *Toronto Directory*, 1856, p. 158; *Canadian Journal*, III (3) June 1855.
7 Province of Canada, *Report on ... Exploration ... between ... Lake Superior and Red River ... 1857* (Toronto, 1858), p. 317.
8 John V. Duncanson, 'W.G.R. Hind, 1833-1888,' *The Hants Journal*, 19 July 1967; *Toronto Normal School, 1847-1897*, p. 200; *Macmillan Dictionary of Canadian Biography* says W.G.R. Hind was drawing master for only two years, not five.
9 Sandford Fleming, 'The Early Days of the Canadian Institute,' *Transactions of the Royal Canadian Institute*, VI, 1899, a semi-centennial memorial volume, pp. 1-24; W.S. Wallace, *The Royal Canadian Institute Centennial Volume, 1849-1949* (Toronto, 1949), pp. 127-129.
10 Wallace, *Royal Canadian Institute*, pp. 129, 138.
11 Royal Canadian Institute, Minutes of the Canadian

Institute, 6 December 1851 and 11 December 1852.
12 Fleming, 'Early Days of the Canadian Institute,' p. 16.
13 G.W. Spragge, 'On Trinity Medical School,' *Ontario History*, LVIII, (2) June 1966, p. 68. Henry Melville, *The Rise and Progress of Trinity College* (Toronto, 1852), pp. 103-104; T.A. Reed (ed.), *A History of the University of Trinity College, 1852-1952* (Toronto, 1952), p. 38.
14 Trinity College, Archives, 'Minutes of the Corporation,' 1 July 1852, p. 103.
15 *Ibid.*, 31 May 1853, p. 140.
16 Trinity College Archives, Written Outline of Lectures in Geology, 1856; also *Trinity College Calendar, 1853, 1854* and *1857*. Hind lectured on General and Organic Chemistry and on Elementary Geology and the Geology of Canada; oddly enough for some time he continued to lecture on the 'Theory of Agriculture,' a bucolic aspect of which one did not suspect even early Trinity College.
17 Wallace, *Royal Canadian Institute*, pp. 181, 185, for Hunt and Chapman.
18 W.E. Logan, *The Geology of Canada* (Montreal, 1863), p. xii.
19 *Canadian Journal*, I (1) August 1852, p. 1.
20 *Ibid.*, II (1) August 1853, p. 1.
21 F.H. Armstrong, 'Metropolitanism and Toronto Re-examined, 1825-1850,' in *Canadian Historical Association, Historical Papers*, 1966, pp. 31-32.
22 Wallace, *Royal Canadian Institute*, p. 142.
23 The attribution of this unsigned article to Hind is by J. Russell Harper in his *Painting in Canada* (Toronto, 1966), p. 140.
24 Queen's University Library, Sandford Fleming, 'Unpublished Diary.' I owe this information to the kindness of Professor Alan Wilson.
25 *Canadian Journal*, III (4) June 1855, p. 398.
26 *Ibid.*, III (1) August 1854; III (2) October 1854.

27 *Ibid.*, New Series, II (xii) November 1857, p. 442.
28 Province of Canada, *Canada at the Universal Exhibition* (Toronto, 1856), pp. 14, 391. The medals included W.E. Logan's grand medal of honour.
29 *Daily Colonist*, 24 January 1857, 21 February 1857; *Canadian Naturalist*, VIII (2), pp. 52-63; *Canadian Journal*, III (2) December 1854, pp. 36-39.
30 Provincial Archives of Ontario, 'Strachan Letter Book, 1854-1862,' p. 95, Strachan to Hind, 23 October 1855.
31 Trinity College, Archives, Hind to College Secretary, 25 October 1855. The notation 'Rec'd and Read' is taken, with the absence of a minute on the subject, to mean that no action was taken.
32 Fleming issued a pamphlet on the survey, *Preliminary Report on the Projected North-West Railway of Canada* (Toronto, 1857). Hind did not contribute to it by name, but it is informed by his spirit of northwestern expansion, and reprints two of his articles from the *Canadian Almanac*, pp. 79-83 and 83-85.

CHAPTER III

1 See A.S. Morton, *A History of the Canadian West to 1870-71* (London, 1939), pp. 825-831; W.L. Morton, *The Critical Years: The Union of British North America, 1857-1873* (Toronto, 1963), pp. 21-34; D.C. Masters, *Rise of Toronto* (Toronto, 1947).
2 The supposition is borne out by Fleming's collaboration with Hind in the latter's *Sketch of an Overland Route to British Columbia* (Toronto, 1862) with an Appendix by Sandford Fleming, 'Practical Observations on the Construction of a Continuous Railroad from Canada to the Pacific Ocean on British Territory.'

3 Irene Spry, *The Palliser Expedition, 1857-1860* (Toronto, 1963) and her edition of the expedition's report in *The Papers of the Palliser Expedition, 1857-1860*, Publications of the Champlain Society, XLIV (Toronto, 1968).
4 Morton, *Critical Years*, pp. 35, 36.
5 McCord Museum, Logan Papers, Hind to Logan, 3 July 1857, a covering letter; Hind to Logan, 3 July, the letter attached.
6 McCord Museum, Logan Papers, Logan to Hind, 7 July 1857.
7 James Richardson, 1810-1883, a Scots farmer of Beauharnois county, interested in geology and employed by Logan. He later became a member of the Survey and worked in the northwest.
8 Province of Canada, *Report on ... Exploration between ... Lake Superior and Red River ... 1857* (Toronto, 1858), p. 5.
9 Public Archives of Canada, R.G.5, C1, vol. 523, a list of the names of the members of the expedition. See also Hind's *Narrative of the Canadian Red River Exploring Expedition of 1857 and of the Assinniboine* [sic] *and Saskatchewan Exploring Expedition of 1858* (London, 1860), I, 3.
10 *Report, 1857*, instructions to Hind, pp. 14-16; also *Narrative*, I, 5-8.
11 Masters, *Rise of Toronto*, p. 66.
12 *Narrative*, I, 12.
13 P.A.C., R.G.5, C1, vol. 523, list of party, Order-in-Council, 18 July 1857.
14 *Narrative*, I, 32; *Report, 1857*, p. 29, Dawson to Provincial Secretary (Terrill), 20 August 1857.
15 P.A.C., R.G.5, S.C1, vol. 579, Hind to Provincial Secretary (Loranger), 31 March 1858.
16 Geological Survey of Canada, *Report, 1847*; Sir John Richardson, *Arctic Searching Expedition* (London, 1851), I.

17 P.A.C., R.G.5, S.C1, vol. 579, John Fleming to Hind, 31 March 1858.
18 P.A.C., R.G.5, C1, vol. 523, Napier to Provincial Secretary (Terrill), 20 August 1857.
19 *Report, 1857*, p. 27, Hind to Terrill, 20 August 1857. Gladman reported that he had secured a guide for the purpose; P.A.C., R.G.5, C1, vol. 523, Gladman to Terrill, 19 August 1857; also, Hind to Terrill, 20 August 1857.
20 *Narrative*, I, 85.
21 *Ibid.*, pp. 96-97.
22 P.A.C., R.G.5, C1, vol. 523, Hind's report, with a section of his journal on the incident at Garden Island and the failure to go by the Roseau to Red River, written from Islington Mission, 30 August 1857; also in *Report, 1857*, pp. 38-53. See *Report*, pp. 116-118, Dawson's account of the incident. *Narrative*, I, 99-100; S.J. Dawson, *Report on the Exploration of the Country between Lake Superior and the Red River Settlement, and between the Latter Place and the Assiniboine and Saskatchewan* (Toronto, 1859), p. 22.
23 *Report, 1857*, p. 121.
24 P.A.C., R.G.5, C1, vol. 523, Hind's Islington report.
25 *Ibid.*; for details see *Report, 1857*, p. 52. Dawson in his *Report* called his disease typhus, p. 12.
26 P.A.C., R.G.5, C1, vol. 523, Hind to the Rev. Robert McDonald, from Fort Garry, 8 September 1957.
27 P.A.C., R.G.5, S.C1, vol. 579, Hind to Terrill, 9 September 1857; Hind to VanKoughnet, 31 March 1858.
28 P.A.C., R.G.5, C1, vol. 523, Gladman's memo on Hind's letter to McDonald of 8 September 1857, undated but early in 1858.

29 P.A.C., R.G.5, C1, vol. 523, Hind to Terrill, St. Paul, 28 October 1857.
30 P.A.C., R.G.5, S.C1, vol. 579, Hind to Terrill, 9 September 1857.
31 For Hind's account of activities in the Red River area see *Narrative*, chapters VI and VII.
32 The reader might wish to see the sketches of Paul Kane made on his journey in the west, now available in J. Russell Harper (ed.), *Paul Kane's Frontier* (Toronto, 1971).
33 *Narrative*, I, 253.
34 *Report, 1857*, p. 61, Hind to Terrill, St. Paul, 28 October 1857.
35 *Narrative*, I, 264; *Globe*, 4 November 1857.
36 *Report, 1857*, p. 64, Hind to Terrill, St. Paul, 28 October 1857. He was later to ask for more time because of difficulty with the illustrations: P.A.C., R.G.5, C1, vol. 523, Hind to Provincial Secretary, 30 November 1857.
37 *Canadian Journal*, New Series, III (xi) March 1858, p. 186.
38 *Report, 1857*, pp. 395-397.
39 *Ontario Archives*, Wm. & S.J. Dawson Papers, William Dawson to Simon, 12 May 1858.
40 P.A.C., R.G.5, S.C1, vol. 579, memo by Wm. Dawson.
41 O.A., Dawson Papers, Simon Dawson to William, 10 April 1858.
42 P.A.C., R.G.5, C1, vol. 523, Gladman to VanKoughnet, 26 January 1858.
43 *Report, 1857*, pp. 159-188, Loranger to Gladman, 30 January 1858.
44 P.A.C., R.G.5, S.C1, vol. 579, Hind to Loranger, 31 March 1858; P.A.C., R.G.5, S.C1, vol. 759, John Fleming to Hind, 31 March 1858. Dickenson to Hind, 1 April 1858.
45 P.A.C., R.G.5, C1, vol. 523, Gladman's memo on Hind's letter.
46 *Report, 1857*, p. 185, Gladman to Loranger, 15 April 1858.

CHAPTER FOUR
1 Henry Youle Hind, *North-West Territory: Reports of Progress together with a Preliminary and General Report on the Assiniboine and Saskatchewan Exploring Expedition* ... (Toronto, 1859), pp. 2, 3. Hereafter cited as *Report*, 1859.
2 P.A.C., R.G.5, S.C1, vol. 579, Hind to Provincial Secretary (Loranger), 24 March 1858.
3 O.A., Dawson Papers, Wm. Dawson to S.J. Dawson, 12 May 1858.
4 P.A.C., R.G.5, S.C1, vol. 579, Hind to Loranger, 10 April 1858. For Hime, see Richard J. Huyda, *Camera in the Interior, 1858* (Toronto, 1975).
5 *Narrative*, I, 274; P.A.C., R.G.5, S.C1, vol. 579, Hind to Loranger, 23 April 1858.
6 *Narrative*, I, 278. See also S.J. Dawson's *Report on the Exploration of the Country between Lake Superior and the Red River Settlement, and between the Latter Place and the Assiniboine and Saskatchewan* (Toronto, 1859), p. 13; P.A.C., R.G.5, S.C1, vol. 579, S.J. Dawson to Loranger, 4 July 1858; also Hind to Loranger, 3 July 1858, announcing his arrival in Red River.
7 *Narrative*, I, 276.
8 These may now be seen in the John Ross Robertson Collection, Metropolitan Toronto Central Library (M.T.C.L.).
9 *Narrative*, I, 296-297.
10 *Report*, 1859, p. 48.
11 *Ibid.*, p. 46.
12 *Ibid.*, p. 56 with map; *Narrative*, I, 366, with map.
13 P.A.C., R.G.5, S.C1, vol. 579, Hind to Loranger, 10 September 1858; M.T.C.L., Hind mss., Hind to T.L. Terrill, 2 February 1859.
14 *Narrative*, I, 334.
15 *Ibid.*, 362.
16 *Report*, 1859, p. 56.

17 John Macoun, *Autobiography, 1831-1921* (Ottawa, 1922), pp. 133-134; Dawson, *Report*, 1859, p. 17, footnote in which he refers to having read Hind's lecture on the subject, and points out that an uncontrolled turning of the Saskatchewan into the Qu'Appelle would drown Red River.
18 *Report*, 1859, p. 83.
19 *Ibid.*, p. 21; Hind to Loranger, 8 November 1858.
20 *Narrative*, II, 37.
21 *Report*, 1859, p. 13; Hind to Loranger, 8 November 1858.
22 *Globe*, 14 December 1858.
23 *Narrative*, II, 82.
24 *Globe*, 28 December 1858.
25 *Canadian Journal*, New Series, IV, July 1859, pp. 253-262. *Toronto Daily Leader*, 7 January 1860.
26 *Toronto Daily Leader*, 12 January 1860.
27 P.A.C., R.G.1, E1, vol. 85, Minutes of Executive Council, 15 April 1861, refusing Hind's request for reimbursement for costs and effort in publication in the United Kingdom of his *Report*.
28 Sir William Edmond Logan, *Geology of Canada* (Montreal, 1863), pp. 11, 214. See also Morris Zaslow, *Reading the Rocks* (Toronto, 1975), pp. 106-107.
29 Warren Upham, *The Glacial Lake Agassiz* (Washington, 1895), pp. 6, 100, 198, 221; John Warkentin, *The Western Interior* (Toronto, 1964), p. 204.
30 Irene M. Spry (ed.), *Papers of the Palliser Expedition, 1857-1860* (Toronto: Champlain Society, 1968), p. 268.
31 M.T.C.L., Hind mss., Hind to Loranger, 2 February 1859.
32 O.A., Dawson Papers, memo by S.J. Dawson, 24 February 1859; F.M. Belcourt to Dawson, 21 January 1860.
33 O.A., Dawson Papers, copy of a document entitled 'The North West,' signed by 'S.J.D.,' and

dated in pencil 29 April 1859.
34 P.A.C., Allan McDonell Papers, Minutes of the North-West Transportation and Navigation Company, 30 August and 22 October 1858; also 13 January 1860. *Globe*, 18 July 1859.
35 *Globe*, 11 May 1858; the Dawsons were, as noted, critical, and with reason, of Hind's conduct in the publication of his report. It is also to be noted that Hind's later connection with Edward Watkin of the Grand Trunk Railway may lend colour to the Dawsons' suspicion.
36 *Globe*, 20 April 1858. For a study of the group, see Donald Swainson, 'The North-West Transportation Company: Personnel and Attitudes,' *Transactions of the Manitoba Historical and Scientific Society, 1969-70*, Series III (26), pp. 59-78.
37 O.A., Dawson Papers, memo by 'S.J.D.,' dated 29 April 1859.
38 Spry, *Palliser Papers*, pp. cxiv-cxv; *Narrative*, I, 1. The origin of the term 'fertile belt' is uncertain and awaits further elucidation by Dr. John Warkentin. It seems to have evolved among Palliser, James Hector, John Arrowsmith, and Hind. See also *Proceedings of the Royal Geographical Society*, V (1861), 201, address on 'Geographical Progress' read by Sir Roderick Murchison, 21 May 1861, in which the term 'fertile belt' was used and described. This was the first authoritative use of the term (courtesy of Dr. John Warkentin).

CHAPTER FIVE
1 The British Museum *Catalogue of Printed Books* notes that there was a second edition of the *Narrative*, but the writer has been unable to discover it, or a reference with its date of publication.

2 P.R.O., C.P. 6/31, Hind to Newcastle, 18 October 1859.
3 P.A.C., G1/49, Newcastle to Sir Edmund Head, 3 November 1859.
4 *Canadian Journal*, New Series, V (xxvi) March 1860, pp. 187-95, 217; *ibid.*, New Series, VI (xxxii) March 1861, p. 196.
5 *Journal of the Royal Geographical Society*, vol. 30, 1860, p. xxx, gives 1860, corrected to 1859 in vol. 34, 1864, pp. 82-87.
6 *Canadian Journal*, New Series, VI (xxxii) November 1861, pp. 175-183. *Edinburgh Review*, CXII, 1861, p. 331.
7 *Journal of the Board of Arts and Manufactures for Upper Canada*, 1861, p. 40.
8 *Canadian Journal*, New Series, VI (xxxii) March 1861, pp. 194-195.
9 *Explorations in the Interior of the Labrador Peninsula, the Country of the Montagnais and Nasquapee Indians*, 2 vols. (London, 1863), I, 10.
10 *Ibid.*, pp. 2-7; J. Russell Harper (ed.), *Paul Kane's Frontier* (Toronto, 1971), pp. 41-42.
11 Public Archives of New Brunswick, Tilley Papers, Hind to Tilley, 6 April 1864.
12 *Labrador*, I, chapter xvi.
13 *Ibid.*, II, 95, 134.
14 *Canadian Journal*, New Series, VII (xxxvii) January 1862, p. 89.
15 Reed, *University of Trinity College*, p. 70.
16 *Canadian Journal*, New Series, VIII (xlviii) November 1863, p. 469.
17 Hind, *Eighty Years' Progress*, p. 33.
18 *British American Magazine*, I, May 1863, 1-11.
19 *British American Magazine*, I, September 1863, p. 559.
20 *Canadian Journal*, New Series, VIII (xlviii) November 1863, p. 415.

21 *British American Magazine*, I, 59-62, 287-99; II, 369-80, 404-8.
22 P.A.C., Watkin Papers, 25, clipping of letter signed 'Canadian,' but here signed by Hind.
23 *Ibid.*, Hind to Watkin, 25 March 1863.
24 *Ibid.*, Hind to Watkin, 4 April 1863.
25 *Ibid.*, Hind to Watkin, 15 July 1863.
26 *Ibid.*, Hind to Watkin, 24 July 1863.
27 *Ibid.*, Hind to Watkin, 27 July 1863; Watkin to Hind, 29 July 1863 (telegram); Hind to Watkin, 29 July 1863 (telegram).
28 *Ibid.*, Hind to Watkin, 27 July 1863.
29 Edward Watkin, *Canada and the United States* (London, 1887), p. 456.
30 P.A.C., Watkin Papers, Hind to Watkin, 28 September 1863.
31 *Ibid.*, Hind to Watkin, 25 March 1863.

CHAPTER SIX
1 *Quarterly Journal of the Geological Society*, January 1864, pp. 122-130; *Canadian Journal*, New Series, IX (1864), 253-262; *Canadian Naturalist*, I (1864).
2 J.W. Bailey, *Loring Woart Bailey: The Story of a Man of Science* (Saint John, 1925) p. 100.
3 Public Archives of New Brunswick, correspondence of S.L. Tilley, Provincial Secretary, Hind to Tilley, 6 April 1864.
4 *Ibid.*, Hind to Tilley, 7 April 1864.
5 Bailey, *Bailey*, p. 87: that Lieutenant-Governor Gordon had done so, presumably from his own pocket, is corroborated in L.W. Bailey, 'Clippings,' kindly supplied to the writer by Dr. A.G. Bailey of the University of New Brunswick.
6 New Brunswick Museum, W.F. Ganong Papers, Bailey to Ganong, 18 December 1917.
7 P.A.N.B., Tilley correspondence, Tilley to Hind, 14 April 1864.

8 *Ibid.*, Tilley to Hind, 9 July 1864.
9 *Ibid.*, Bailey to A.H. Gillmor, Jr., 15 May 1865.
10 Archives, Trinity College, Minutes of Corporation, 18 May 1864.
11 *Ibid.*, 11 October 1864.
12 Public Archives of Ontario, Strachan Letter Book, 1851-66, p. 17, draft testimonial for Hind, 30 August 1864.
13 Hind, *A Preliminary Report on the Geology of New Brunswick together with a Special Report on the Distribution of the 'Quebec Group' in the Province* (Fredericton, 1865), pp. ix-xi; N.B.M., Hind's field notebooks, no. 1.
14 Queen's University Archives, Sandford Fleming Papers, Fleming to Mrs. Fleming, 28 August 1864.
15 P.A.N.B., Tilley correspondence, Hind to Tilley, 29 August 1864.
16 *Ibid.*, Hind to Gillmor, 15 May 1865; Tilley to Bailey, 26 November to 20 December 1864.
17 N.B.M., Ganong Papers, Bailey to Ganong, 15 December 1917.
18 *Ibid.*, Bailey to Ganong, 23 April 1918.
19 *Ibid.*
20 Bailey, 'Clippings.'
21 N.B.M., *Journal of the Assembly of New Brunswick*, 1865, pp. 109, 117, 144; also P.A.N.B., Provincial Secretary, Gillmor to Bailey, 13 May 1865.
22 Hind, *Preliminary Report*; L.W. Bailey, G.F. Matthew, and H.C. Hartt, *Observations on the Geology of Southern New Brunswick* (Fredericton, 1865), 162 pp. with coloured map.
23 Hind, *Preliminary Report*, p. 96.
24 *American Journal*, XL, 142.
25 Bailey, *Bailey*, p. 101 explicitly declares Hind a plagiarist.
26 Logan warned Robb in 1868 against Hind's propensity to plagiarize, and castigated the Rev. D. Honeyman for not reporting, when employed by the Geological Survey, a geological discovery

of Honeyman's which Logan implies Hind had appropriated; Geological Survey, correspondence, letter books, Logan to Robb, 24 July 1868, and to Honeyman, sometime in 1870.
27 Public Archives of Nova Scotia, Hind Papers, Fleming to Hind; for the Logan references to Hind's *Preliminary Report* see the 2nd edition of Dawson's *Acadian Geology*, 1866.
28 R.W. Ells, *A History of New Brunswick Geology* (Montreal, 1887) pp. 14-58.
29 Hind, *Preliminary Report*, chapters 2, 8, 9.
30 Logan, *The Geology of Canada*, chap. 21, pp. 670-877.
31 Public Archives of Canada, G21/101, A.J. Smith, Minister of Fisheries, to Premier of Newfoundland, 24 April 1877.
32 Wm. G. MacFarlane, *New Brunswick Bibliography* (Saint John, 1895), p. 44.
33 P.A.N.S., *Hants Journal*, 'Death of Dr. Henry Youle Hind's Son,' 10 August 1865.
34 Smithsonian Institution, Official Correspondence, vol. 58, Hind to Joseph Henry, 28 August 1865; King's College, *King's College Calendar, 1865-66*, p. 45.
35 Windsor, Hants Court Registry, vol. 4, Entry 857/0.
36 *Ibid.*, Entry 1871.

CHAPTER SEVEN
1 Windsor, *Hants Journal*, 12 August 1908.
2 Nova Scotia Historical Society, *Collections*, vol. 34, 1963, Gwendolyn V. Shand, 'The Industries of Nova Scotia'; Hind, *Report on the Property of the Mineral Exploration and Mining Association of Nova Scotia*.
3 The pamphlets are listed in the Bibliography.
4 The reports on the *Waverley Gold District*, the *Nova Scotia Gold Districts*, and the *Cumberland Coal Field* were authorized by the government of

Nova Scotia. On the value of Hind's work on the gold fields, see Nova Scotia, House of Assembly, *Journals*, 1870, 'Mines Report,' p. 5.

5 Geological Survey, Records, Selwyn to Meredith, 3 January 1871; he was in touch with Hind but doubtful of employing one 'well known' to be speculating in mines and mineral lands. See also McCord Museum, Logan Papers, Logan to Honeyman, undated but immediately after November 1869; I owe this reference to Professor M. Zaslow. Bailey, *Bailey*, p. 101.

6 Nova Scotia Historical Society, *Collections*, G.R. Evans, 'Early Gold Mining in Nova Scotia,' vol. 25, 1938.

7 *Nature*, vol. 10, May-October 1874.

8 *Frank Leslie's Illustrated Newspaper* (New York) 26 February 1881, p. 431. Hind refers to Ellerhausen in his 'Notes on some Geological Features of the North Eastern Coast of Labrador,' *Canadian Naturalist*, 13, 6 April 1877. I am indebted for personal information on Ellerhausen to Dr. C.B. Fergusson, late Provincial Archivist of Nova Scotia. The Ellerhausen family home is still a landmark near Halifax.

9 Queen's University, Archives, Fleming Papers, Hind to Fleming, 8 May 1876.

10 'On the Influence of Anchor Ice in Relation to Fish Offal and the Newfoundland Fisheries' (St. Johns, 1877); Public Archives of Nova Scotia, Hind Papers, 'The Migration of the Harp Seal' (unpublished).

11 *Frank Leslie's Illustrated Newspaper*, 26 February 1881, p. 431.

12 P.A.N.S., Hind Papers, undesignated mss. entitled, 'Vol. 1. The Fisheries of British North America.' *Ibid.*, Macmillan & Co. to Hinde [sic], 29 January 1878.

13 P.A.C., G21 /101, Smith to Premier of Newfoundland, 24 April 1877.

14 H.Y. Hind, *The Effect of the Fisheries Clauses of the Treaty of Washington on the Fishers and Fisheries of British North America* (Halifax, 1877).
15 Halifax Commission, *Documents and Proceedings*, III, 3399-3443.
16 *Frank Leslie's Illustrated Newspaper*, 26 February 1881, p. 431.
17 J.S. Dennis, 'Introduction,' *Navigation of Hudson's Bay* (Ottawa, n.d. but Introduction dated 11 November 1878).
18 P.A.C. G21/101, Macdonald to de Winter, 24 February 1879; Heather Gilbert, *Awakening Continent* (Aberdeen, 1965) p. 8, fn.
19 A memorandum prepared by W.F. Whitcher of the Department of Fisheries, and laid before the Commons in March 1880. It was not published in *Sessional Papers* and was destroyed by the fire of 1916.
20 PAC, Macdonald Papers, Galt to Macdonald, 16 February 1880.
21 Montreal *Gazette*, 15 January 1881, Halifax *Morning Chronicle*, 7 April 1881, Hind to Governor General. The principal publications of Hind in the controversy are listed in the Bibliography.
22 P.A.N.S., Hind mss. So much may be deduced from an undated personal note from George Johnson of the Department of Agriculture, Ottawa, with a note on Hind (missing) for 'The Journal' and one from Sandford Fleming (also missing). As Johnson was at the department from 1887 to 1891, his note must have been written within that period.
23 Hind, *An Exposition of the Fisheries Commission Frauds*, p. 32. Smithsonian Institution, Official Correspondence, vol. 106, Spencer Baird to Hind, 17 January 1881. Baird later expressed surprise at the attacks on Hind; he had not, Baird could say 'with great truth,' 'attempted to make any

money out of the United States in this connection.' *Ibid.*, 3 June 1881. See also C.C. Tansill, *Canadian-American Relations, 1875-1911* (Toronto, 1943) p. 12, where he points out that no reasons were given by the commission for the award, and that the amount was thought excessive in the United States.
24 Personal interview with Mrs. Claude R. Smith, Windsor, 1968.
25 Somerset House Registry, 1885, H., p. 347.
26 H.Y. Hind, *Centennial History of the University of King's College, Windsor, Nova Scotia, 1790-1890* (New York, 1890). King's College, *Calendar*, 1890-1891.
27 King's College, *Calendar*, 1886-1887, and 1887-1888; P.A.N.S., *McAlpine's City Directory*; the unusual name is Hungarian.
28 P.A.C., M.G.29, G27, vol. 9, H.J. Morgan clipping on Hind-Sumichrast libel suit, 1887; *Acadian Recorder*, 26 May 1887.
29 Halifax, *Morning Herald*, 27 May 1887; *Morning Chronicle*, 28 May 1887.
30 P.A.N.S., *Calendar of the Church School for Girls*, Windsor, Nova Scotia, 1891-92; for history of Edgehill, see Mildred H. Roechling, *Memories of Edgehill, 1891-1966*.
31 Halifax *Herald*, 10 August 1908.
32 P.A.N.S., Church School for Girls, *Calendar*, 1892-1893, p. 33.
33 Windsor, *Hants Journal*, 12 August 1908.
34 Court of Probate, County Court House, Windsor, will of Henry Youle Hind.
35 County Court House, Windsor, Registry of Deeds, 1941.
36 *Science*, New Series, XXV, 222 (no. 716), 18 September 1908, p. 370. F.V. Hayden and A.R.C. Selwyn, *Geography of North America* (London, 1883), p. 381; H.M. Ami, *North America, Canada and the United States* (London, 1915), 1, p. 407.

Bibliography

OFFICIAL REPORTS

Province of Canada

Report on a topographical and geological exploration of the canoe route between Fort William, Lake Superior, and Fort Garry, Red River; and also of the valley of the Red River, north of the 49th parallel, during the summer of 1857 (Toronto, 1858). Also published by the Imperial Government as *Papers relative to the exploration of the country between Lake Superior and the Red River Settlement* (London, 1859).

North-West Territory: Reports of progress; together with a preliminary and general report on the Assiniboine and Saskatchewan exploring expedition, made under instructions from the Provincial Secretary, Canada (Toronto, 1859). Also published by the Imperial Government as *British North America Reports of Progress,* ... (London, 1860) with reproduction of photographs.

New Brunswick

A preliminary report on the geology of New Brunswick together with a special report on the distribution of the "Quebec Group" in the Province (Fredericton, 1865).

Documents and proceedings of the Halifax Commission, 1877, under the Treaty of Washington of May 8, 1871 (Halifax, 1877), 3 vols., I-III. (Hind, as 'curator' of the minutes and papers of the Commission, supervised the printing of this collection.)

BOOKS

Narrative of the Canadian Red River Exploring Expedition of 1857 and of the Assiniboine and Saskatchewan Exploring Expedition of 1858 (London, 1860), 2 vols. (There is said to be a 2nd edition but I have been unable to find it.)

A Sketch of an Overland Route to British Columbia, with an appendix (Toronto, 1862).

Explorations in the Interior of the Labrador Peninsula, the Country of the Montagnais and Nasquapee Indians, 2 vols. (London, 1863).

Eighty Years' Progress of British North America (Toronto, 1863). Edited and in part written by Hind, with special articles by others; republished with additions as *The Dominion of Canada, with an appeal for its protection, ornamentation and preservation* (Toronto, 1869).

Sketch of the Old Parish Burying Ground of Windsor (Windsor, N.S., 1889).

Centennial History of the University of King's College, Windsor, Nova Scotia (Windsor, N.S., 1890).

PAMPHLETS

Lectures on Agricultural Chemistry (Toronto, 1850).

A Comparative View of the Climate of Western Canada (Toronto, 1851).

Essay on the Insects and Diseases Injurious to Wheat Crops (Toronto, 1857).

Report of the Waverley Gold District (Halifax, 1868).

Notes on the Structure of Nova Scotia Gold Districts (Halifax, 1869).

Report on the Sherbrooke Gold District together with a paper on the Gneisses of Nova Scotia and an abstract of a paper on the Gold Mining in Nova Scotia (Halifax, 1870).

Report on the Strawberry Hill Mine (Halifax, 1870).

Report on the Sydney Colliery, Cape Breton (Halifax, 1871).

A Sketch of the Mineral Resources of Part of Cumberland County (Halifax, 1872).

Report on the Point Acoui Coal Property, Sydney Coal Field, Cape Breton (Halifax, 1872).

Report on the Mount Uniacke, Oldham, and Renfrew Gold Mining Districts (Halifax, 1872).

Report on the Topographical Survey of the Cumberland Coal Field with Notices of the Coal Seams and their Relation to the Iron Deposits of the Cobequids (Halifax, 1873).

Report on the Property of the Mineral Exploration and Mining Association of Nova Scotia (Halifax, 1873).

A Forecast of the Future of the Maritime Provinces (Saint John, 1876).

The Importance of an Knowledge of Rock Foldings to Miners (Saint John, 1876), 2nd ed. (Windsor, N.S., 1902).

Report on the Petroleum Indications at Chevrie, Hants County, Nova Scotia (Sussex, N.B., 1901).

The Effect of the Fisheries Clauses of the Treaty of Washington on the Fishers and Fisheries of British North America (Halifax, 1877).

Correspondence Respecting the Presence of Falsified Statistics in the Case of Her Majesty's Government, presented at Halifax (Halifax, 1879).

Falsisifed Departmental Reports: A Letter to His Excellency the Marquis of Lorne, Governor General of Canada (Windsor, N.S., 1880).

Letter to the Rt. Hon. Earl of Kimberley, Nov. 5, 1881 (n.p. 1881).

Emigration, Land and Railway Frauds: An Outcome of the Lambeth Conference of 1878, Exemplified in a Letter to His Grace, the Archbishop of Canterbury ... (Windsor, N.S., 1882).

A Letter on Misrepresentation Concerning the North-West Territories of the Dominion of Canada as a Field of Emigration and Investment (Nottingham, 13 April 1882).

The Corruption of the Geological Survey in the North-West Territories Matters (n.p., 1883).

Manitoba and the North-West Frauds: Correspondence with the Department of Agriculture ... Rejecting the Impostures of Professor John Macoun and Others (Windsor, N.S., 1883).

An Exposition of the Fisheries Commission Frauds, showing how the frauds were concealed by the use of the number 666, and the masking numbers 42, 10, 7, 2, taken from the 13th chapter of Revelation (Windsor, N.S., 1883).

Besides the above there are numerous individual letters to the press.

ARTICLES and PAPERS

"Notes on the Geology of Toronto," *Canadian Journal*, I, February 1853), pp. 147-151.

"Report on the Preservation and Improvement of Toronto Harbour," *Canadian Journal*, Supplement, 1854.

"The Future of Western Canada," *Canadian Almanac*, 1856.

"Our Railway Policy," *Canadian Almanac*, 1857.

"The Possible Use for the Manufacture of Illuminating Gas of the Utica Shales Near Collingwood," and "Minerals of Canada," two lectures given before the Mechanics' Institute of Toronto, 1857. *Daily Colonist*.

"The Great North-West," *Canadian Almanac*, 1858.

"Of Some of the Superstitions and Customs Common among the Indians in the Valley of the Assiniboine and Saskatchewan," *Canadian Journal*, New Series, IV (July 1859), 253-262.

"North-West British America," by the editor (Hind), *British American Magazine*, I, May-June, 1863.

"Salmon-spearing in Labrador by Torch Light," by the editor (Hind), *British American Magazine*, I, May 1863.

"Sketches from Indian Life," *British American Magazine*, I, May 1863.

"What Is Spectrum Analysis?" *British American Magazine*, I, Aug. 1863.

"On the Cultivation and Manufacture of Flax and Hemp in Canada." *British American Magazine*, I, Aug-Sept. 1863.

"The Labrador," *British American Magazine*, I, Oct. 1863.

"A Glance at the Political and Commercial Importance of Central British America," *Canadian Journal*, New Series, VIII (November 1863), pp. 409-427.

"The Political and the Commercial Importance of the Fisheries of the Gulf of St. Lawrence, Labrador and Newfoundland," *British American Magazine*, I, Nov. 1863.

"Heat and Motion - a New Philosophy," *British American Magazine*, I, Dec. 1863.

"Observations on Supposed Glacial Drift in the Labrador Peninsula, Western Canada, and on the South Branch of the Saskatchewan," *Quarterly Journal of the Geological Society*, XX, 30 Jan. 1864; *Canadian Journal*, New Series, IX (July 1864), pp. 253-262; and *Canadian Naturalist*, New Series, I, 1864.

"On Two Gneissoid Series in Nova Scotia and New Brunswick," *Nature* and *Quarterly Journal of the Geological Society*, 1874.

"On the Laurentian and Huronian Series in Nova Scotia," *American Journal*, XLIX' 1874.

"The Figure of the Earth in Relation to Geological Inquiry," *Nature*, vol. 10, May-Oct. 1874.

"Notes on Some Geological Features of the North Eastern Coast of Labrador," *Canadian Naturalist*, New Series, vol. 8, 1878.

"Notes on the Fishing Grounds of Northern Labrador," *Canadian Naturalist*, New Series, vol. 8, 1878.

PAPERS READ

"On the North American Drift," Canadian Institute, Feb. 1855.

"A Practical Introduction to a Mode of Manufacturing Gun Cotton," Canadian Institute, Feb. 1855.

"On the Origin of the Basin of the Great Lakes," Canadian Institute, March 1855.

"On the Blue Clay of Toronto," Canadian Institute, March 1856.

"The Distribution of Clay Iron-Stone in the Cretaceous Rocks of Rupert's Land in the North-West Territory," Canadian Institute, 1859.

"On the Occurrence of Grasshoppers in the Northwest," Canadian Institute, April 1860.

"Remarks on Indian Art, illustrated by a collection of Indian relics obtained during the Assiniboine and Saskatchewan Expeditions," Canadian Institute, Jan. 1861.

"On the Manufacture of Shale Oil from the Utica Slate of Collingwood," Canadian Institute, Feb. 1861.

"A Communication Embodying Observations Made during His Expedition to the Labrador Coast in the Summer of 1861," Canadian Institute, Dec. 1861.

"On Vegetable Parchment, Its Uses and Preparation," Canadian Institute, Autumn 1863.

"On the Influence of Anchor Ice in Relation to Fish Offal and the Newfoundland Fisheries, 1877.

"The Migration of the Harp Seal," Provincial Archives of Nova Scotia, Hind Papers.

"Comparison between the British North American Fisheries and Those of Other Countries," Provincial Archives of Nova Scotia, Hind Papers.

Index

Agassiz, Louis, 99, 125
albertite, 107, 109
Allan, G.W., 75
American Journal, 115, 139
Ami, H.M., 126
Anderson, Bishop David, 52
Assiniboine River, 49, 62, 63
Atlantic fisheries, 91, 117

Bailey, Professor L.W., 101-2, 104-9
Bellecourt, Rev. G.A., 42
Bell, Alexander Graham, 124
Betts Cove Copper Mine (Nfld.), 116
Big Ridge (Man.), 47, 62-3
Bigsby, Dr. J.J., 4
Binney, Bishop Hibbert, 124
Black, Rev. John, 46
Blodget, Lorin, 54
Bourgeaux, Eugene, 40
Bovell, Dr. James, 19
British American Magazine, 94-95
British Colonist, 14
Brown, George, 28, 97
Budd, Rev. Henry, 69
Bunn, Dr. John, 44

Bury, Lord, 78-97
Butler, William, 8, 10, 16, 117

Cambridge University, 11
Canadian Almanac, 26, 29
Canadian Institute, Royal, 18-19, 21, 23-24, 53, 75, 83-84, 86, 91-3, 99, 123
Canadian Journal, 19, 22-24, 75, 83-85, 94, 99, 121, 128
Canadian Naturalist, 99
Canadian Pacific Railway, 116, 119-20, 121
Cavendish, Lord Frederick, 74, 97, 119
Cayley, Edward, 34, 52, 87
Chapman, Edward John, 21, 24, 82
Choné, Jean-Pierre, 37
Confederation, 93-95, 98
Crees, Plains, 67-68, 75
Croft, Henry Holmes, 21, 82
Cumberland, Frederic William, 18

Dawson, John William, 99, 106-8, 115
Dawson, Simon James, 34, 37, 38-45, 50, 52, 54, 55-57, 58-59, 61, 68, 103-5, 109
Dawson, William Macdonell, 54-56, 80-81, 84
Delfosse, Baron, 118
Dennis, John Stoughton, 18
Dickenson, J.A., 34, 45, 52, 55, 59, 62, 66, 70-71, 74-75
Dilke, Sir Charles Wentworth, 121

Edgehill School for Gilrs, 113, 125
Ellerhausen, Francis, 116
Ells, R.W., 109

Ferland, Abbé J.B.A., 86
Fertile Belt, 70, 78, 81, 116
Fisheries Award (1871), 119-20
Fleming, John, 35, 38, 49, 51, 52, 55-56, 59, 63, 69, 71-72, 75

Fleming, Sandford, 18, 21, 28, 36, 103-4, 116-17, 121
Flett, George, 48
Fort Ellice, 65-66, 70, 91
Fort Frances, 37-39, 61
Fort Garry, Upper, 43-49
Fort William, 36-37

Galt, Sir Alexander Tilloch, 118, 120
Ganong, W.F., 106
Garden Island (Ont.), 39, 40-41, 46, 50
Gaudet, G.F., 34, 44, 52, 87
Geological Society, London, 99, 115
Geological Survey of Canada, 25, 31-33, 60, 77, 114, 119-20, 122
Geology of Canada (Logan), 77, 109
Gesner, Abraham, 105
Girton House (Halifax), 124-25
Gladieux, Pierre, 59-60
Gladman, George, 34-35, 35-36, 40-41, 43-46, 47-48, 52, 55-57, 66, 71-74
Gladman, Henry, 34
Globe, 14, 18, 28, 34, 54, 80-81
Gowler, Oliver, 48-49, 51
Gunn, Donald, 46

Halifax Award, 119, 121
Halifax Fisheries Commission, 117-19
Hartt, H.C., 104
Hayden, F.V., 126
Headquarters, The, 105-6
Henry, Joseph, 110
Hime, Humphrey Lloyd, 59, 66, 70-71
"Hind Charges," 119-21
Hind, James Fisher, 6, 10, 111-12
Hind, John Russell, 9-10
Hind, Katherine, 126
Hind, Katherine Cameron, 16, 113-14
Hind, Margaret, 125

Hind, Sarah, 6
Hind, Sarah Youle, 3, 5
Hind, Thomas Sr., 3, 5, 7, 8, 9
Hind, Thomas Jr., 6, 10
Hind, William G.R., 6, 17, 87, 92, 126
Hodder, Dr. E.W., 19
Honeyman, Rev. Dr. D., 111, 114
How, Rev. Henry, 111
Hudson's Bay Company, 29-30, 38, 44, 46-47, 80-81, 97, 120
Humboldt, Alexander von, 11, 125
Hunt, Thomas Sterry, 26, 82

Illustrated London News, 59
Islington Mission (Ont.), 42-44

Journal of the Board of Arts and Manufactures for Upper Canada, 86

Kellogg, E.H., 118
Killaly, H.H., 34
King's College, 110-11, 113, 123

Labrador, 87-90, 116-17, 118
Leipzig, 10˜ Oeffentliche Handelslehranstalt, 10, 11, 13
Lefroy, John, 97
Lillie, A.R., 43, 56
Logan, (Sir) William Edmond, 18, 21, 25-26, 31-33, 39, 77-79, 82, 100, 103, 108-9, 114, 123
Loranger, T.J., 55

Macdonald, (Sir) John A., 30, 120
McDonald, Rev. Robert, 42-43, 45, 56
McDermot, Andrew, 46-47
Macdonell, Allan, 36-79
McGee, Thomas D'Arcy, 94, 97, 125
McIntyre, Chief Trader John, 37
McKay, John W., 65

Macoun, John, 68, 76, 119
Mactavish, Chief Factor William, 44, 46, 56
Matthew, G.F., 77, 101, 104, 106-9
Maury, M.F., 125
Mechanics' Institute (Toronto), 26
Mineral Exploration and Mining Association of
   Nova Scotia, 114
Mitchell, Hon. Peter, 100
Moisie River, 86-88, 91
Montagnais, 91-92
Murchison, Sir Roderick, 30, 100
Murray, Alexander, 38

Napier, W.H.E., 34, 38, 47, 52
Naskapis, 90
Nature, 115
New Brunswick Geological Survey, 100, 102, 107-9
Newcastle, Henry Pelham Fiennes Pelham-Clinton,
   Duke of, 83-84, 95-96
Newfoundland, 117
Northcote, Sir Stafford, 120
North Shore (St. Lawrence), 87
Northwest, exploration of, 26, 29-30, 36, 79-80,
   82, 116, 126
North-West Transportation Company, 80, 97
Nottingham, 3-7, 11
Nottingham Free Grammar School, 81
Nottingham Journal, 72

Ojibwas (Lake of the Woods), 40-42

Palliser, Captain John, 30, 38, 78, 83, 84
Palliser's Triangle, 65
Pembina, 49, 53
Pembina Escarpment, 63
Pether, Postmaster Robert, 38-40
Portage la Prairie, 46-47, 82
Pratt, Charles, 65

Qu'Appelle River, 65-68, 89
Qu'Appelle Mission, 65
Quebec Group, 109, 115

Red River, valley of, 30, 43, 54, 78
Red River Settlement, 45-56
Richardson, James, 32, 77-80
Richardson, Sir John, 38
Riding Mountain, 72-73
Robb, Professor James, 105
Robertson, Thomas Jaffray, 13-16, 57
Robinson, Henry, 115
Roseau River, 50
Roseau River Portage, 32, 39-40, 43, 51, 56
Royal Geographical Society, 30, 84
Russell, S.L., 34, 52, 60
Ryerson, Egerton, 12-14

St. Paul, 50, 53, 61
Salaberry, Charles de, 35, 45
Saskatchewan River, 54, 66, 69, 71, 83
Science, 126
Select Committee of Enquiry, 1857 (British). 30
Select Committee of Enquiry, 1857 (Canadian), 30, 34
Selwyn, A.R.C., 126
Settee, Rev. James, 65
Simpson, Sir George, 38, 52, 58-59
Smithsonian Institution, 46, 110, 115, 121
Smith, Hon. (Sir) Albert J., 105-12, 119
Souris River, 32, 47, 64, 75
Spence, John, 47
Strachan, Bishop John, 19, 27-28, 102
Sumichrast, F.C., 124-25
Sunnyside (Windsor, N.S.), 112-13, 122, 125-26

Taylor, J.S. ('Saskatchewan'), 63
Taylor, James Wickes, 94
Terrill, T.L., 45, 53

Thompson, Harriet, 4, 72
Tilley, Hon. Samuel Lenoard, 100-6
Toronto, 11, 15, 17, 23, 29, 79; Provincial Normal School, 19
Trinity College, University of, 19-21, 27, 31, 75, 83, 86, 91-93, 98-99, 102, 113; Medical School, 19

Universal Exhibition, Paris (1877), 117
University College (University of Toronto), 21, 24
Upham, Warren, 77

Vankoughnet, Hon. Philip, 31

Washington, Treaty of (1871) 117-19
Watkin, Edward, 96-99, 123-26
Wells, A.M., 34, 43-45, 52, 68
Whitcher, W.F., 119-21
Wilson, Daniel, 23
Windsor (N.S.), 110-13, 122, 125
Wynne, Robert, 34, 38

Young, Edward, 119

OGLER LIBRARY